Everyday SEL in Early Childhood

With this bestselling book from educational consultant Carla Tantillo Philibert, you'll gain practical strategies for teaching Social Emotional Learning (SEL), mindfulness, and well-being to help improve the human connection between you and your students. You'll find out how to lead students through mindfulness activities, simple yoga poses, and breathwork techniques. Topics include mindful practices, well-being strategies to combat stress and anxiety, giving your students the space to understand their emotions and strengthen peer-to-peer communication, developing the foremost and essential SEL competencies, and engaging in experiential activities to strengthen social emotional skills. The new edition reflects the latest CASEL guidelines and includes updated activities, as well as a brand-new directory of terms, and an intentional focus on educators' and students' socio-emotional well-being. Perfect for early childhood educators at any level of experience, the book will help you develop positive youth identity and promote connectedness so students can deal successfully with life's stressors beyond school doors.

Carla Tantillo Philibert is the founder of Mindful Practices, one of the Midwest's leading Social Emotional Learning and well-being organizations. Mindful Practices is a team of dedicated members who share SEL, mindfulness, and well-being practices with school communities across the globe to improve the human connection between students and educators. Carla and her husband, Rob, also co-created the SEL check-in platforms Class Catalyst (for students) and Five to Thrive (for families), along with SEL On Demand, a curated catalog of SEL video content.

**Also Available from
Carla Tantillo Philibert and Routledge**
www.routledge.com/k-12

Everyday SEL in Elementary School, Second Edition:
Integrating Social Emotional Learning and Mindfulness
Into Your Classroom

Everyday SEL in Middle School, Second Edition:
Integrating Social Emotional Learning and Mindfulness
Into Your Classroom

Everyday SEL in High School, Second Edition:
Integrating Social Emotional Learning and Mindfulness
Into Your Classroom

Everyday Self-Care for Educators: Tools and Strategies for
Well-Being
With Christopher Soto and Lara Veon

Everyday SEL for Administrators
With Allison Slade

Everyday SEL in the Virtual Learning Classroom
With Allison Slade

Everyday SEL in Early Childhood
Integrating Social Emotional Learning and Mindfulness
Into Your Classroom
Second edition
Carla Tantillo Philibert

Everyday SEL in Early Childhood

Integrating Social Emotional Learning and Mindfulness Into Your Classroom

Second edition
Carla Tantillo Philibert

NEW YORK AND LONDON

Second edition published 2022
by Routledge
605 Third Avenue, New York, NY 10158

and by Routledge
2 Park Square, Milton Park, Abingdon, Oxon, OX14 4RN

Routledge is an imprint of the Taylor & Francis Group, an informa business

© 2022 Taylor & Francis

The right of Carla Tantillo Philibert to be identified as author of this work has been asserted by her in accordance with sections 77 and 78 of the Copyright, Designs and Patents Act 1988.

All rights reserved. No part of this book may be reprinted or reproduced or utilised in any form or by any electronic, mechanical, or other means, now known or hereafter invented, including photocopying and recording, or in any information storage or retrieval system, without permission in writing from the publishers.

Trademark notice: Product or corporate names may be trademarks or registered trademarks, and are used only for identification and explanation without intent to infringe.

First edition published by Routledge 2017

Library of Congress Cataloging-in-Publication Data
Names: Tantillo Philibert, Carla, author.
Title: Everyday SEL in early childhood : integrating social-emotional learning and mindfulness into your classroom / Carla Tantillo Philibert.
Other titles: Everyday social-emotional learning in early childhood
Description: Second Edition. | New York : Routledge, 2021. | "First edition published by Routledge 2017"—T.p. verso. | Includes bibliographical references and index.
Identifiers: LCCN 2021001725 (print) | LCCN 2021001726 (ebook) | ISBN 9780367692209 (Hardback) | ISBN 9780367692216 (Paperback) | ISBN 9781003140948 (eBook)
Subjects: LCSH: Affective education. | Reflective teaching. | Emotional intelligence. | Social learning—Study and teaching (Early childhood)
Classification: LCC LB1072 .T358 2021 (print) | LCC LB1072 (ebook) | DDC 370.15/34—dc23
LC record available at https://lccn.loc.gov/2021001725
LC ebook record available at https://lccn.loc.gov/2021001726

ISBN: 978-0-367-69220-9 (hbk)
ISBN: 978-0-367-69221-6 (pbk)
ISBN: 978-1-003-14094-8 (ebk)

Typeset in Palatino
by Apex CoVantage, LLC

Dedication

For Rob, my loving muse, patient husband, and supportive thought partner.

Contents

Foreword	ix
Acknowledgments	xi
Meet the Author	xiii
Directory of Terms	xvii
Introduction	1
1 An Approach, Not a Program	9
2 Three Steps for Getting Started	29
3 Pre-Teaching for Success	43
4 SEL-Informed Classroom	55
5 Framing SEL	67
6 Implementation and Integration	72
7 SELF (Intrapersonal) Practices	74
Yoga Sequence 1: Seated Arm Stretch and Starfish Pose	75
Yoga Sequence 2: Mountain Pose, Starfish Pose, and Seated Arm Stretch	77
Yoga Sequence 3: Mountain Pose, Tippy Toes Breath, and Tree Pose	79
Draw and Rip	81
Listening Breath	83
Happy Note	84
Memory Minute	85
Tap Our Worries Away	86
Cotton Ball Breath	87
Equal Breath	88
Lion's Breath	89

8 SOCIAL (Interpersonal) Practices	**91**
Color Breath	92
Bee's Breath	93
Positive Paperchain	94
Compliment Partners	96
Pass the Animal	97
Kind Kid Postcard	98
Community-Based Service Learning Project	99
9 Crafting SEL Stories	**100**
10 Recruiting Your Administrator	**106**
Appendix	**113**
Educator Pre-/Post-Self-Assessment	113
Educator Questions From the Field	115
Bibliography	**121**

Foreword

Dottie Nola and Remi Philibert, 5 and 3 years old

In the five years since the first editions were released, I have become a parent of two small children. When I tried the strategies within the pages of those first editions with my own peanuts at home, sometimes they worked beautifully. And, sometimes they didn't. When the activities did not work as planned, I would ask the opinions of the resources that were sitting right in front of me: my own kids.

I believe that SEL, as a discipline, has made a few key mistakes. The largest is that we have forgotten to listen to the children who are practicing the strategies. If SEL is going to be both relevant and sensitive to the needs of today's youth, adults need to stop guessing what children are thinking and feeling and pause to take the time to ask them. Then, listen.

The following is a transcribed interview I conducted of Dottie Nola (5-and-a-half years old) and Remi (almost 3 years old) on Social Emotional Learning, cool down strategies, and why managing feelings can sometimes be hard. As you implement SEL and mindfulness in your classroom, and perhaps your home, I encourage you take a moment to ask the youth you serve what they think and feel about the skills you are asking them to practice. What works? What doesn't? Why? Not only will this inform your work as a practitioner, but it will also demonstrate to your students (and children at home) that their voices matter and by using their words they can positively influence how the world around them operates.

> **Me:** What is Social Emotional Learning?
> **Dottie Nola:** It is expressing your feelings.
> **Remi:** It is when you cry and then you are learning.
> **Me:** Why is it important to talk about your feelings?
> **Dottie Nola:** So then other kids or people can help you fix it. Let's pretend that I was scared because Remi had climbed a high tree. I had found him on a high tree. If you tell people that you are scared then they can help you solve the mystery of your feelings and get the happiness back.
> **Me:** How do you solve the mystery of feelings, Dottie Nola?

Dottie Nola: You try to play a song and dance to it. Make yourself have a unicorn face with a unicorn mask. You can play dress-up or you can pretend that you are swimming with turtles. Or, do an animal walk. (She hops up to demonstrate an animal walk.) Breathing is the last good thing that helps. I think the breathing helps you mind what is bothering you and you calm down. And then you can dance to your favorite song.

Me: What do we do when our feelings are out of control? Or, we feel angry or mad?

Remi: (Sticks his tongue out and makes raspberries.) My tongue is out! I run or jump or slide. Jump into water. Put your clothes on your head. (Dottie Nola laughs.)

Dottie Nola: Remi, you can't put your clothes on your head! If I feel like I am going to have a fit or a fight, I am not silly. I stomp like a big, angry giant. So, I don't let the feelings hurt me. You've got to be strong and feel how it feels to have all those emotions inside your heart. Like colors. I draw a picture. Paint. If I have negative emotions I stop them in a special way that only I know.

Me: What is the special way that only you know, Dottie Nola?

Dottie Nola: It's a secret. (She steps close to me to whisper.) Do the stuff you want to do. The things that make you feel like you want to calm down. Like if you are in school and you feel angry. Do something that is fun in the school or tell your teacher that you are angry.

Remi chimes in: When I am angry I dance because there is ants in my pants.

—Dottie Nola and Remi Philibert, November 2020

Acknowledgments

I must begin by acknowledging that the path outlined inside this book borrows ideas from some of the most thoughtful and innovative work in the fields of mindfulness, yoga, culturally responsive and anti-racist teaching practices, pediatrics, Cognitive Behavioral Therapy (CBT), trauma-informed practices, somatics, and theater games. Along with insights from thought leaders such as qualitative yoga researchers Andrea Hyde and Catherine Cook-Cottone; Peter Senge on systems thinking in schools; Brené Brown on vulnerability; Gretchen Rubin on happiness; Ronald D. Siegel and Jon Kabat-Zinn on mindfulness; Weissburg, Jennings, Greenberg, and Durlak; CASEL on Social-Emotional Competence (SEC); California's CORE districts on evidence-based SEL implementation; Charlotte Danielson's teaching framework (most notably Domains 1 and 2); Doug Lemov's classroom management strategies; Harry Wong's warm, organized classroom; and practices to build relational trust gleaned from John Hattie's work.

There are so many kind and compassionate folx in my life who are part of this book's journey. Rob, Dottie Nola, and Remi, thank you for patiently giving me the space to learn how to juggle (albeit clumsily) being a wife, mother, leader, and author. Additionally, many thanks to Auntie Cathy, Auntie Precious, Nana, my mother, Violet, and my dear father, Pat, for the gifts of your time, love, and childcare!

My mentor, the inspiring Paul Liabenow and his beautiful wife, Bonnie, have welcomed me into their Michigan family with generosity and warmth. Their patience, faith, and love have been invaluable to me and my family these past three years.

I give a proud nod to my Mindful Practices team who helped me design, implement, and refine some of the activities contained in this book. I am indebted to Erika Panichelli, Mindful Practices' hard-working Director of Operations. Our Mindful Practices family has been indispensable in sharing their wisdom, ideas, and feedback for the activities included within. I am humbled every day by the experience of leading such a hard-working, dedicated, and innovative team. Stefanie Piatkiewicz and Vienna Webb have shared their magical talents and insights to make the SEL activities on these pages both accessible and engaging. Kate Alfonzo and Ericka Byrne shared their amazing tools while Erin Daugherty and Erika Haaland also provided great insights when assisting with edits for the new edition.

I thank my valued friend and research partner, Dr. Kiljoong Kim, for the gift of his guidance and wisdom. He has been instrumental on the journey to deepen the strength and quality of our SEL programming.

As for the book itself, I am immensely grateful to Mindful Practices' many fabulous partners across the country for opening your doors and sharing your amazing school communities with us. You have truly given us a home to take risks and learn together!

To my amazing mother—thank you for gently forcing me to write my first book. (Per usual, you were right.) And thank you to Mom, Dad, and our dear friend Mary Kusper, who helped me assemble that first edition in our basement with the help of a plastic comb binding machine. Mom and Dad, I am forever in your debt for all you have done for me and Mindful Practices.

I am swimming in gratitude for my warm, thoughtful, and encouraging editor, Lauren Davis, and the Routledge family. I am honored to write for such a supportive publishing house and for you, the readers, who have purchased this book and supported SEL and mindfulness in schools. Many of you have reached out with thoughts, questions, or feedback and have shared these resources with your district leadership. Your support cannot be measured with words. Thank you!

Most of all I thank my loving husband, Rob, a sleep-deprived father, tech innovator, and team leader. His encouragement, creative input, and patience with my "This is the final draft, I promise!" speech gave me the space to reflect and grow as a writer, mother, and partner. Rob, you are the love of my life. Your positive impact knows no bounds.

Meet the Author

Carla Tantillo Philibert founded Mindful Practices in 2006 to share innovative Social Emotional Learning (SEL), mindfulness, and well-being with thousands of students, educators, and families nationwide. A certified yoga teacher with a master's degree in curriculum and instruction, Carla has taught at both the secondary and elementary levels. Carla was a founding teacher and curriculum director of a high school in Chicago's Little Village community, is the co-creator of Hip-HopYoga™, and is the co-founder of the student check-in platforms Class Catalyst and Five to Thrive. Carla is also co-creator of Michigan Public Television's POP Check series. Carla is a highly qualified professional development facilitator, keynote speaker, and author of *Cooling Down Your Classroom: Using Yoga, Relaxation and Breathing Strategies to Help Students Learn to Keep Their Cool* (2012), the *Everyday SEL Series* (Elementary, 2016; Middle School, 2016; and High School, 2017), and *Everyday Self-Care for Educators: Tools and Strategies for Well-Being (2019)*. Carla is also a contributing author for *Stories of School Yoga: Narratives from the Field* (2019) and *Educating Mindfully: Stories of School Transformation Through Mindfulness* (2020). Carla and her husband, Rob, have two amazing children, Dottie Nola and Remi, and the family enjoys long adventure walks around Chicago neighborhoods with their black lab, Ralphie.

About Our Offerings

EdTech SEL Solutions

SEL implementation can be tough—there is never enough *time*! I wanted to harness the time-saving power of technology to help educators connect with more kids.

So, I recruited my husband, Rob, with his background in all things Internet (user experience, coding, and online product development). He used his expertise to digitize our practices and strategies to help adults connect one-on-one with students. Together we built prototypes, beta tested concepts, and integrated insights from our research partner, Dr. Kiljoong Kim at Chapin Hall at the University of Chicago, to create evidence-based EdTech SEL solutions for your classrooms.

- **Class Catalyst**: SEL Check-In Platform (EC - HS)

  What: A student-centered platform for connecting students with a caring adult through daily check-ins.

  How: A simple check-in to allow students to report on how they are feeling and provide them with individualized practices to be present.

  When: Once a day for 3 minutes to practice Self-Awareness and build relational trust with a caring adult.

  SEL Focus: Self-Awareness, Self-Regulation, Voice, Agency, Positive Youth Identity, Human Connection and Relational Trust.

- **Five to Thrive**: SEL Check-In Platform for parents and children

  What: A student-centered platform that connects families at home.

  How: Simplified check-ins, which can be done independently or with the support of a caregiver or parent.

  When: Once a day for 5 minutes to practice Self-Awareness and build relational trust with a caring adult.

  SEL Focus: Self-Awareness, Self-Regulation, Voice, Agency, Positive Youth Identity, Human Connection and Relational Trust.

- **SEL On Demand**: Curated Catalog of SEL Videos

  What: An online catalog of SEL videos broken down by grade band (from EC to HS) and duration.

  How: Teachers access the video library to find engaging SEL videos varying in length and current topics, such as managing anxiety or anger.

  When: Daily, as needed.

SEL Focus: Self-Awareness, Self-Regulation, Social Awareness, Balance between Social Harmony and Self-Efficacy.

To schedule a free demo of any of our EdTech SEL solutions, please email Rob at hello@classcatalyst.com.

As you dive into the book, please don't hesitate to contact me with questions or inquire about our online (live or recorded) and in-person professional learning, coaching, and workshop opportunities. I absolutely love hearing from educators, administrators, and parents. Email me directly at carla.p@mindfulpractices.us.

Directory of Terms

1. *Agency*: Student agency refers to learning through activities that are meaningful and relevant to learners, driven by their interests, and often self-initiated with appropriate guidance from teachers. To put it simply, student agency gives students voice and often, choice, in how they learn. Their ability to make a decision triggers a greater investment of interest and motivation.
   SOURCE: "Student Agency." *Renaissance EdWords*. https://www.renaissance.com/edwords/student-agency/. Accessed March 2, 2021.

2. *Anti-racism*: The active process of identifying and eliminating racism by changing systems, organizational structures, policies and practices, and attitudes so that power is redistributed and shared equitably.
   SOURCE: *The National Action Committee on the Status of Women International Perspectives: Women and Global Solidarity.* University of Massachusetts Amherst, Office of the Provost website, 2021. https://www.umass.edu/provost/resources/all-resources/faculty-diversity/anti-racism-resources

3. *Anti-racist Pedagogy*: A paradigm within Critical Theory utilized to explain and counteract the persistence and impact of racism praxis as its focus to promote social justice for the creation of a democratic society in every respect.
   SOURCE: Blakeney, A. M. (2011). Antiracist Pedagogy: Definition, Theory, Purpose, and Professional Development. *Journal of Curriculum & Pedagogy* 2(1), 119–132.

4. *Authentic Student Voice*: The student voice is made up of the thoughts, views, and opinions of students on an educational journey. Engaging all students, not just those who volunteer regularly, to use their voices to incorporate their knowledge, life experiences, and cultures allows students to authentically lead, make decisions, and solve problems. Authentic student voice is an asset for all school communities.
   SOURCE: *CASEL Guide to Schoolwide SEL*, 2021. https://schoolguide.casel.org/focus-area-3/school/elevate-student-voice/

5. ***Breath Work***: Conscious, controlled breathing done especially for relaxation, meditation, or therapeutic purposes.
SOURCE: Breath Work. *Merriam-Webster.com Dictionary*. https://www.merriam-webster.com/dictionary/breath%20work. Accessed February 25, 2021.

6. ***Compassion***: Sympathetic consciousness of others' distress together with a desire to alleviate it. Self-compassion refers to the ability to turn understanding, love, and acceptance inward toward oneself.
SOURCES: "Compassion." *Merriam-Webster.com Dictionary*, Merriam-Webster, https://www.merriam-webster.com/dictionary/compassion. Accessed March 2, 2021.
"Self-Compassion." *GoodTherapy.org,* GoodTherapy, https://www.goodtherapy.org/learn-about-therapy/issues/self-compassion. Accessed March 2, 2021.

7. ***Consciousness***: Consciousness refers to your individual awareness of your unique thoughts, memories, feelings, sensations, and environments. Essentially, your consciousness is your awareness of yourself and the world around you. This awareness is subjective and unique to you, and is constantly shifting and changing. If you can describe something you are experiencing in words, then it is part of your consciousness.
SOURCE: Cherry, K. (2020). "Theories: Cognitive Psychology: What Is Consciousness?" *Very Well Mind*. https://www.verywellmind.com/what-is-consciousness-2795922

8. ***Culturally Responsive Teaching***: A pedagogy that recognizes the importance of including students' cultural references in all aspects of learning. Culturally responsive teaching acknowledges, responds to, and celebrates fundamental cultures and offers full, equitable access to education for students from all cultures. Some of the characteristics of culturally responsive teaching are:
   1. Positive perspectives on parents and families
   2. Communication of high expectations
   3. Learning within the context of culture
   4. Student-centered instruction
   5. Culturally mediated instruction
   6. Reshaping the curriculum
   7. Teacher as facilitator

   SOURCE: Ladson-Billings, G. (1994). *The Dreamkeepers*. San Francisco, CA: Jossey-Bass Publishing Co.

9. ***Digital and/or Remote Learning***: Digital, or remote, learning provides an opportunity for students and teachers to remain connected and engaged with the content while working from their homes. Opportunities for remote learning are typically linked to emergency situations that pose a threat to student safety. It is important to note that in remote learning environments, versus virtual learning environments, the learner and teacher are not accustomed to having distance during instruction. This may pose a challenge to both teacher and learner that can be accommodated for through specific support structures. Remote learning is different from virtual school or virtual learning programs that typically have gone through an official process of establishing a school, adopting an online curriculum, and creating a dedicated structure to support students enrolled in the school. eLearning utilizes electronic technologies to access educational curriculum outside of the traditional classroom.
SOURCE: Ray, K. (2020). *"Remote Learning Playbook."* https://www.techlearning.com/news/remote-learning-playbook-free-special-report-from-tech-and-learning

10. ***Dysregulation***: Dysregulation, also known as emotional dysregulation, refers to a poor ability to manage emotional responses or to keep them within an acceptable range of typical emotional reactions. This can refer to a wide range of emotions including sadness, anger, irritability, and frustration. While emotional dysregulation is typically thought of as a childhood problem that usually resolves itself as a child learns proper emotional regulation skills and strategies, emotional dysregulation may continue into adulthood.
SOURCE: Cuncic, A. (2021). "Emotions: What Is Dysregulation?" *Very Well Mind*. https://www.verywellmind.com/what-is-dysregulation-5073868

11. ***EdTech***: A term combining "education" and "technology" that refers to hardware and software designed to enhance teacher-led learning in classrooms and improve students' education outcomes.
SOURCE: Frankenfield, J. (2020). "EdTech." *Investopedia*. https://www.investopedia.com/terms/e/edtech.asp

12. ***Educators***: A collective term for employees working within a school or district who have direct interaction with students, including teachers, paraprofessionals, aides, coaches, instructors, specialists, etc.
SOURCE: Mindful Practices, 2021.

13. *Human Connection*: An energy exchange between people who are paying attention to one another. It has the power to deepen the moment, inspire change, and build trust. At Mindful Practices, this often involves play, communication, and collaboration.
    SOURCE: Pisacano Brown, D. (2018). "The Power of Human Connection." *LI Herald*. https://www.liherald.com/stories/the-power-of-human-connection,102632

14. *Instructional Time*: The amount of time during which learners receive instruction from a classroom teacher in a school or a virtual context. Intended instructional time is usually specified in school or education policies or regulations.
    SOURCE: International Bureau of Education, UNESCO. 2013.

15. *Intentionality*: Deliberate action to move past tendencies. The opposite of "responding on autopilot" or falling back into the same narrative. This requires disciplined habits of mind. Ownership.
    SOURCE: Mindful Practices. (2021).

16. *Interpersonal*: Being, relating to, or involving relations between persons.
    SOURCE: "Interpersonal." *Merriam-Webster.com Dictionary*, Merriam-Webster, https://www.merriam-webster.com/dictionary/interpersonal. Accessed March 2, 2021.

17. *Intrapersonal*: Occurring within the individual mind or self.
    SOURCE: "Intrapersonal." *Merriam-Webster.com Dictionary*, Merriam-Webster, https://www.merriam-webster.com/dictionary/intrapersonal. Accessed March 2, 2021.

18. *LGBTQIA2S+*: An acronym for Lesbian, Gay, Bisexual, Transgender, Queer and/or Questioning, Intersex, Asexual, Two-Spirit, and the countless affirmative ways in which people choose to self-identify.
    SOURCE: Portland Art Museum. https://portlandartmuseum.org/learn/programs-tours/object-stories/powerful-self-lgbtqia2s-lives-today/

19. *Meditation*: To engage in contemplation or reflection; to engage in mental exercise (such as concentration on one's breathing or repetition of a mantra) for the purpose of reaching a heightened level of spiritual awareness.
    SOURCE: "Meditate." *Merriam-Webster.com Dictionary*, Merriam-Webster, https://www.merriam-webster.com/dictionary/meditate. Accessed February 25, 2021.

20. *Mindfulness*: "The awareness that emerges through paying attention on purpose," Jon Kabat-Zinn.
    Mindfulness means maintaining a moment-by-moment awareness of our thoughts, feelings, bodily sensations, and surrounding environment, through a gentle, nurturing lens. Mindfulness also involves acceptance, meaning that we pay attention to our thoughts and feelings without judging them—without believing, for instance, that there's a "right" or "wrong" way to think or feel in a given moment. When we practice mindfulness, we are tuning our thoughts into what we're sensing in the present moment rather than rehashing the past or imagining the future.
    SOURCE: "Mindfulness Defined: What is Mindfulness?" *Greater Good Magazine*, 2021. https://greatergood.berkeley.edu/topic/mindfulness/definition

21. *Mindful Practices*: The interplay between interpersonal and intrapersonal SEL skill development and how the practices of vocalization, movement, stillness, and human connection,
    or what we call Mindful Practices develop not only one's Self-Awareness but, in turn, an increased ability for one to form positive connections with others.
    SOURCE: Mindful Practices (2021).

22. *Movement*: Physical motion between points in space. It is the combination of the physicality of skill development combined with the artistry of self-expression. Conceptually, movement is organized as Space, Time, Force, and Body. At Mindful Practices, we consider movement to involve yoga, dance, fitness, and stretching.
    SOURCE: Green Gilbert, A. (1992). *Creative Dance for All Ages*, 2nd Edition. Champaign, IL: linois

23. *Native and Indigenous Peoples*: Also referred to as First peoples, Aboriginal peoples, or autochthonous peoples, are ethnic groups who are native to a particular place on Earth and live or lived in an interconnected relationship with the natural environment there for many generations prior to the arrival of non-Indigenous peoples.
    SOURCE: "Indigenous Peoples." In Wikipedia. https://en.wikipedia.org/wiki/Indigenous_peoples. Accessed February 25, 2021.

24. *Non-instructional Time*: Time set aside by the school before actual classroom instruction begins or after actual classroom instruction ends.

SOURCE: 20 USCS § 4072 (4) Title 20. Education; Chapter 52. Education for Economic Security; Equal Access. https://definitions.uslegal.com/n/noninstructional-time-education/

25. *Non-judgmentalness*: Noticing yourself (thoughts, words, deeds) and the world around you without evaluation, appraisal, assessment or the need to label (actions, feelings or emotions) *good* or *bad*. Clarity.
SOURCE: Mindful Practices. (2021).

26. *People of Color (POC)*: Often the preferred collective term for referring to non-white racial groups. Racial justice advocates have been using the term "people of color" (not to be confused with the pejorative "colored people") since the late 1970s as an inclusive and unifying frame across different racial groups that are not white, to address racial inequities. While "people of color" can be a politically useful term, and describes people with their own attributes (as opposed to what they are not, e.g., "non-white"), it is also important whenever possible to identify people through their own racial/ethnic group, as each has its own distinct experience and meaning and may be more appropriate. Some people choose to capitalize "People of Color," while others choose not to; while there is not a "correct" capitalization rule, it is most often a term that is seen capitalized.
SOURCE: Race Forward, *Race Reporting Guide*. (2015). The Center for Racial Justice Innovation. https://www.raceforward.org/reporting-guide

27. *Positive Youth Identity*: Identity refers to how one defines themselves in terms of values, beliefs, and their role in the world. Self-identity in adolescence forms the basis of our self-esteem later in life. Youth identity is the result of various internal and external factors. The development of clear and positive identity/identities involves building self-esteem, facilitating exploration of and commitment to self-definition, reducing self-discrepancies, and fostering role formation and achievement.
SOURCE: Watson, J., Aspiro Adventure, and Tsang, S. K. M., Hui, E. K. P., & Law, B. C. M. Positive Identity as a Positive Youth Development Construct: A Conceptual Review. *The Scientific World Journal*, Article ID 529691, 8 pages. https://doi.org/10.1100/2012/529691

28. *Practices*: To perform (an activity) or work at (a skill) repeatedly so as to become proficient. At Mindful Practices, we consider these

practices to be in connection with Self-Awareness, movement, mindfulness, regulation, etc.
SOURCE: "Practice." *Merriam-Webster.com Dictionary*, Merriam-Webster, https://www.merriam-webster.com/dictionary/practice. Accessed February 25, 2021.

29. *School Connectedness*: School connectedness is the belief held by students that adults and peers in the school care about their learning as well as about them as individuals. Students are more likely to engage in healthy behaviors and succeed academically when they feel connected to school. School connectedness is particularly important for young people who are at increased risk for feeling alienated or isolated from others. Those at greater risk for feeling disconnected include students with disabilities, LGBTQIA2S+ students, students who are homeless, or any student who is chronically truant due to a variety of circumstances. Strong family involvement and supportive school personnel, inclusive school environments, and curricula that reflect the realities of a diverse student body can help students become more connected to their school.
SOURCE: "School Connectedness." (2014). American Psychological Association. https://www.apa.org/pi/lgbt/programs/safe-supportive/school-connectedness

30. *School Stakeholders*: Typically refers to anyone who is invested in the welfare and success of a school and its students, including administrators, teachers, staff members, students, parents, families, community members, local business leaders, and elected officials such as school board members, city councilors, and state representatives. Stakeholders have a "stake" in the school and its students, meaning that they have personal, professional, civic, or financial interest or concern.
SOURCE: *"Stakeholder."* (2014). The Glossary of Education Reform. https://www.edglossary.org/stakeholder/

31. *Self-Awareness*: The abilities to understand one's own emotions, thoughts, feelings, and values and how they influence behavior across contexts, including impact on one's physical self. This includes capacities to recognize one's strengths and limitations with a well-grounded sense of confidence and purpose, as well as the ability to take ownership for the emotions you have and understand your power of choice in response to those emotions.

SOURCE: "SEL: What Are the Core Competence Areas and Where Are They Promoted?" (2020). CASEL website. https://casel.org/sel-framework/

32. *Self-Management or Self-Regulation*: The abilities to manage one's emotions, thoughts, and behaviors effectively in different situations and to achieve goals and aspirations. This includes the capacities to delay gratification, manage stress, and feel motivation and agency to accomplish personal/collective goals.
SOURCE: "SEL: What Are the Core Competence Areas and Where Are They Promoted?" (2020). CASEL website. https://casel.org/sel-framework/

33. *Singularity*: The ability to focus on a single task at hand; the opposite of multitasking. Being fully present and engaged with one thing at a time. Space to learn and hear what our bodies are telling us. Awareness.
SOURCE: Mindful Practices. (2021).

34. *Social Awareness*: The abilities to understand the perspectives of and empathize with others, including those from diverse backgrounds, cultures and contexts. This includes the capacities to feel compassion for others; understand broader historical and social norms for behavior in different settings; and recognize family, school, and community resources and supports.
SOURCE: "SEL: What Are the Core Competence Areas and Where Are They Promoted?" (2020). CASEL website. https://casel.org/sel-framework/

35. *Social Emotional Competence (SEC)*: The ability to interact with others, regulate one's own emotions and behavior, solve problems, and communicate effectively.
SOURCE: "Social-Emotional Competence of Children: Protective and Promotive Factors." (2018). Center for the Study of Social Policy. https://cssp.org/wp-content/uploads/2018/08/HO-2.1e-CW-Social-Emotional-Competence.pdf

36. *Self-Efficacy and Social Harmony*: When in balance, the learner feels centered, present, and like a valued and contributing member of the world around them. This competency also reflects the learner's ability to find their voice and to use actionable insights to balance the needs of the self with the needs of others without excessive self-sacrifice.

37. *Social Emotional Learning (SEL)*: The process through which all young people and adults acquire and apply the knowledge, skills, and attitudes to develop healthy identities, manage emotions and achieve personal and collective goals, feel and show empathy for others, establish and maintain supportive relationships, and make responsible and caring decisions. SEL advances educational equity and excellence through authentic school-family-community partnerships to establish learning environments and experiences that feature trusting and collaborative relationships, rigorous and meaningful curriculum and instruction, and ongoing evaluation. SEL can help address various forms of inequity and empower young people and adults to co-create thriving schools and contribute to safe, healthy, and just communities.
SOURCE: *"SEL is. . ."* (2020). CASEL website. https://casel.org/what-is-sel/

38. *SEL-Informed Classroom*: being informed about, sensitive to and making time to practice Social Emotional Learning, an adaptive environment for students and adults in which their Intrapersonal (SELF) and Interpersonal (SOCIAL) needs are in balance.

39. *Social (or Socio) Emotional Well-Being*: Healthy social, emotional, and behavioral well-being is defined as a child's developing capacity to:

    ◆ Form close, secure, meaningful relationships
    ◆ Experience, regulate, and express emotions
    ◆ Explore the environment and learn new skills

    SOURCE: "Social Emotional Well-Being." (2019). The Kaleidoscope Project. https://www.kaleidoscopewake.org/social-emotional-well-being

40. *(Creating) Space*: Creating mental, emotional, and physical marginality in your life. The space to respond compassionately to different personal and social triggers without losing one's center or sacrificing social rapport. The opposite of dysfunctional *groupthink* or habitual, unconscious reactions to everyday events. Consciousness.
SOURCE: Mindful Practices. (2021).

41. *Stillness*: A state of freedom from storm or disturbance; quietness; silence; calmness. Mindful Practices often refers to stillness reached through meditation, reflection, breath work, and/or mindfulness. Stillness of the body does not necessarily mean the mind is still—our

thoughts still persist. However, continued stillness of the body can lead to stillness of the mind.
SOURCE: "Stillness." *Merriam-Webster.com Thesaurus*, Merriam-Webster, https://www.merriam-webster.com/thesaurus/stillness. Accessed February 25, 2021.

42. **Students (Young People) Who Have Experienced Trauma**: A traumatic event is a frightening, dangerous, or violent event that poses a threat to a child's life or bodily integrity. Witnessing a traumatic event that threatens the life or physical security of a loved one can also be traumatic. This is particularly important for young children as their sense of safety depends on the perceived safety of their attachment figures. Traumatic experiences can initiate strong emotions and physical reactions that can persist long after the event. Traumatic events can occur outside of the family (such as a natural disaster, car accident, school shooting, or community violence) or within the family (such as domestic violence, physical or sexual abuse, or the unexpected death of a loved one).
SOURCE: "About Childhood Trauma." The National Child Traumatic Stress Network. https://www.nctsn.org/what-is-child-trauma/about-child-trauma

43. **Trauma-Informed Practices**: A trauma-informed practice is defined as an organizational structure and treatment framework that involves understanding, recognizing, and responding to the effects of all types of trauma.
SOURCE: "Becoming a Trauma-Informed Practice." *American Academy of Pediatrics*. https://www.aap.org/en-us/advocacy-and-policy/aap-health-initiatives/resilience/Pages/Becoming-a-Trauma-Informed-Practice.aspx

44. **Trauma-Informed Systems**: A trauma-informed child and family service system is one in which all parties involved recognize and respond to the impact of traumatic stress on those who have contact with the system including children, caregivers, and service providers.
SOURCE: The National Child Traumatic Stress Network

45. **Vocalization**: To express oneself or use the voice to articulate a need, issue, or thought. Can be through speaking, chanting, singing, or other forms of sound.

SOURCE: "Vocalize." *Merriam-Webster.com Dictionary*, Merriam-Webster, https://www.merriam-webster.com/dictionary/vocalize. Accessed February 25, 2021.

46. *Voice*: In education, student voice refers to the values, opinions, beliefs, perspectives, and cultural backgrounds of individual students and groups of students in a school, and to instructional approaches and techniques that are based on student choices, interests, passions, and ambitions.
SOURCE: "Student Voice." *The Glossary for Education Reform*, updated December 12, 2013. https://www.edglossary.org/student-voice/

47. *Vulnerable Learners*: A student or someone who has no access or limited access to basic needs such as sufficient and nutritious food, shelter, adequate clothing, a safe home and community environment free from abuse and exploitation, family care and support, good healthcare, and the ability to take full advantage of available education opportunities.
SOURCE: Bialobrezeska, M., Randell, C., Hellmann, L., Winkler, G. (2009). *"Creating a Caring School: A Guide and Toolkit for School Management Teams."* South African Institute for Distance Education (SAIDE). https://www.saide.org.za/documents/Toolkit.pdf

48. *Well-Being*: The experience of health, happiness, and prosperity. It includes having good mental health, high life satisfaction, a sense of meaning or purpose, and the ability to manage stress. More generally, well-being is just feeling well, happy, healthy, socially connected, and purposeful.
SOURCE: Davis, T. (2019). "What Is Well-Being? Definition, Types, and Well-Being Skills." *Psychology Today*. https://www.psychologytoday.com/us/blog/click-here-happiness/201901/what-is-well-being-definition-types-and-well-being-skills

49. *Yoga*: A system of physical postures, breathing techniques, and sometimes meditation derived from the Hindu theistic philosophy of Yoga that is often practiced independently, especially in Western cultures, to promote physical and emotional well-being.
SOURCE: "Yoga." *Merriam-Webster.com Dictionary*, Merriam-Webster, https://www.merriam-webster.com/dictionary/yoga. Accessed February 25, 2021.

Introduction

> Our aim is to fully awaken our heart and mind, not just for our own greater well-being but also to bring benefit, solace, and wisdom to other living beings. What motivation could top that?
> Pema Chödrön (2020)

The field of SEL has grown significantly in the five years since we published the first edition of *Everyday SEL*. With alarming rates of school shootings, student suicides, incidents of racial injustice, and absenteeism, we have a moral imperative to not only do this work but to also do it *better*. If these systemic issues in our country continue to persist we must be continually looking inward and asking ourselves how SEL can make a greater impact. Business as usual with SEL implementation is not good enough, clearly. We must fully awaken both heart and mind, as Chödrön so eloquently states.

The positive feedback for the first editions warmed my heart. However, given how SEL keeps growing in importance, it was time for a refreshed edition for each grade band. My editor and I worked through pieces that readers were craving such as adding a directory of terms, simplifying some of the activities, adding a few new practices, and including an intentional focus on educators' and students' socio-emotional well-being. We also wanted this book to provide our readers with resources to develop positive youth identity and to promote school connectedness, two critical components to any classroom's SEL approach.

I hope that you not only find these additions responsive to your needs as the boots-on-the-ground folx working with students each day but also that this perspective—one that prioritizes your well-being at the top of the conversation—is motivating. Motivating for you and passionate, dedicated educators like you to find your voice and speak your Adult SEL needs loud and proud.

On average, my organization, Mindful Practices, works with about 75 schools and districts in the United States and Latin America each year. These schools vary in size, resources, and demographic makeup. However, there are two problems I see consistently: a lack of focus on Adult SEL and well-being (emotionally exhausted educators are asked to address the emotional needs of children) and that SEL is happening *to* students, not *with* students. Adults are assessing SEL mastery without taking the time to regularly hear from the students, in their own words, what their SEL needs are and without giving them the space to cultivate Self-Awareness, voice and agency.

I have been practicing SEL and mindfulness in schools since 2006. Truth is, it all starts with us, the adults. Our well-being, our Self-Awareness, our willingness to dive into *the work*. And when I say *the work*, I don't mean burning hours putting together Google docs on SEL or sitting on committees. Yes, that *is* work. But *the work*, is the work that we do getting to know ourselves and our lens and biases. Cultivating our Self-Awareness, without judgment, so that we know what our well-being needs are and we know how to meet them. The temptation is to focus first on the SEL standards, dive into PD trainings, set up task forces, and comb through data. While those are all valuable pursuits, unless we set aside time and space to explore the well-being needs of the educators—those caring adults and school stakeholders (teachers, paraprofessionals, administrators, counselors, social workers, clerks, etc.) who teach our youth how *to be* in the world—we are merely placing a Band-Aid on the gushing wound of compassion fatigue, burnout, and workplace stress that is currently plaguing the educational system. Doing *the work* is about making time to take care of ourselves, not just because we deserve it (which we do), not just because we will be more emotionally available for our students (which we will), not just because it will improve our interpersonal relationships with our colleagues (which it will), but because the power of compassionate human connection is why we are here doing *this work*.

As educators with limited time (and often the guilt that comes with spending time on ourselves) one question may be, how does taking care of ourselves connect to the power of compassionate human connection? When we take the time to practice self-care, we get to know ourselves and our needs and what is needed to meet those needs. We can more readily care for ourselves with a non-judgmental, compassionate lens and, in turn, can see our students and their needs with that same lens.

I am beginning this book with a focus on intentional Adult SEL and well-being. As the old adage goes, the children in a classroom are only as regulated as the adult at the front of the room. As said by my friend and co-author Chris Soto in our book, *Everyday Self-Care for Educators* (Philibert, Soto, and Veon, 2020):

> There is a sense of unease that the national reports of teacher stress may be a canary in the coal mine regarding public education. Teachers are at the heart of the very mission of public schools—providing a social and economic safety net for our democratic institutions through access to quality learning opportunities. That so many of them report high levels of stress and low levels of job satisfaction should precipitate both data-informed reflections on the most common symptoms and research-based approaches towards the most effective solutions . . . emphasiz(ing) the importance of awareness and self-advocacy in light of these distressing trends.
> (Soto & Veon, 2020)

In *Everyday Self-Care for Educators,* Chris moves on to discuss how systems that do not prioritize educator well-being will often see a negative impact in "the culture of the classroom and the learning of individual students, most often by harming the learning connection between student and teacher."

Understanding, of course, that well-being is not accessible to all of us in the same way. And, if we live in a country that prioritizes education we should also live in a country that prioritizes the well-being of our educators. As Maurice Swinney, the Chief Equity Officer of Chicago Public Schools points out, we must look critically about how we talk about educator self-care and whether or not it is a practice that is accessible for all.

> Take care of yourself is what people say. For many People of Color, self-care may show up differently. Self-care for me is releasing myself from feeling like I have to live up to whiteness. Being successful at wellness . . . as an African American man, a Black man, living in white dominated culture proved more difficult than one might think. There were pressures—a series of undue burdens—to be a Black man who represents all things Black. Whether pressed upon me or self-imposed, room for vulnerability or opportunities to make mistakes were minimal. I wanted to always do my best work, reminding myself that the temporary anguish is worthy of the outcome. But I also knew that longevity would only occur if I created space to acknowledge my

moods, thoughts, and wonderings. Over time, wellness became the thing I had to gift myself to continue to serve my school community, specifically my students.

Keeping both Dr. Soto's and Dr. Swinney's words in mind, let's ask ourselves, after academics, what is the purpose of anything we devote time to during the school day? How much time do we devote to developing a compassionate connection with ourselves and the students we serve?

To help students grow into people who have positive relationships and can lead lives of agency and choice, don't we need to demonstrate that we also have the agency to take care of our well-being needs? Devoting valuable classroom time to well-being and SEL practices is a way to empower our students with the life-long learning tools that will serve them long into adulthood, such as being self-aware and collaborative, while it also gives us the space to practice taking care of ourselves. When we think of creating space, this is where mindfulness comes into play. Through mindfulness practices, or tools that help us pay attention on purpose in the present moment, we are better able to find the space to explore our needs, biases, emotions and reactions.

When I work with schools across the globe to develop sustainable SEL and mindfulness programs, I often kick off our initial professional development (PD) session with a question: If you were to bump into a former student at the grocery store, what is the number one thing you would like to learn about them or hear them say?

Almost all educators respond that they want their former students to be "happy and healthy," which leads us into a discussion of the importance of taking the time to teach and model well-being and SEL, so that students have those life skills into adulthood. Occasionally, I will hear an educator say, "Right, but . . . I didn't sign up to teach this touchy-feely stuff. It is not *my* job. Students should be learning this stuff at home." And, of course, we all agree to a point. Yes, our students *should* be learning social and emotional skills at home, but they should also have the chance to learn and practice SEL skills in *many* different environments and contexts, especially if we are hoping that they take root for a lifetime. Being able to possess Self-Awareness, sit with and regulate emotions and feelings, and effectively communicate and build relationships can only be learned through trial and error, and most importantly, practice. School happens to be a place where children and young adults spend the majority of their day, and therefore, schools have a great opportunity and a responsibility to help students build these critical life skills. Let's all make time for well-being and SEL in our classrooms and view a student's ability to deal successfully with life's stressors as our litmus test for impact.

Thoughts for Educators

You work hard. You give your all each day. Please take a moment to prioritize your well-being. It is critically important not only for your students but for you. Take time to cultivate your Self-Awareness. Understand what your needs are and how to meet those needs, even during a packed school day. Then, decide where SEL will fit into that packed day. What reinforces the interpersonal relationship that you have with your students? What brings you and your students into greater connection (POP Chart check-ins, Thumb Checks, etc.) during non-instructional time? In parallel, when do you explicitly teach SEL content during instructional time to provide students with words and contexts they need to give depth and breadth to their understanding?

Aim for your SEL approach to include non-instructional time, building intentional, interpersonal relationships between adults and students (educators getting to know kids) *and* giving students the space to get to know themselves (Self-Awareness) outside of academics. Also, think about resources/kits/curricula you can use during instructional time to explicitly teach the SE competencies and embed SEL content into academic instruction.

When working with teachers across the country, I often hear the question, "Why is Winfred so well behaved for Ms. Munoz and has such a difficult time in my class?" I refer to this trend as *teacher magic*: when a teacher intuitively adapts their instruction to meet the needs of a child, but the strategies were never explicitly taught to that student and they exit that classroom without an improved sense of Self-Awareness. Often these students leave school without the words to identify what positively or negatively impacts their learning or an awareness of how they learn best. Our job is to create space for students to guide the conversation about their learning. Let's educate students about why, as their teachers, we make certain choices about their learning and why it is important that they weigh in as to whether or not those choices worked.

The Mindful Practices SE competencies—Self-Awareness, Self-Regulation, Social Awareness, and the balance between Self-Efficacy and Social Harmony—many teachers possess simply by virtue of being nurturers and educators. These competencies are often intuitive, as strong educators understand what students need and shift the energy of their classroom accordingly. However, some of the best teachers I have observed, when asked, cannot put their practices into words. While these teachers are effective managers of their classrooms, without the words to explain their methodology, students may excel in their class and struggle in the next. The techniques in this book provide the tools to put practices into words.

Given the emphasis on teacher Self-Awareness, this approach necessitates that we leave our comfort zones. This is not a program with the singular focus of merely knocking SEL off a to-do list or only practicing on Wednesday at 2:15 pm. Instead, it is an integrated approach that calls on teachers and school stakeholders to be present and reflective. SEL programs that rely heavily on teachers reading scripted scenarios do not reinforce Adult SE competence (or SEC), or build positive relationships between students and teachers. It is one thing to read a prompt to a student and another to create space during non-instructional time to build an interpersonal relationship with that student *and* to have the SEC and content knowledge to address their needs in real-time.

Sure, scripted kits are easier. One hundred percent. But, if they were working, our suicide rates for students (and teachers) would not continue to rise year after year. Let's be real about the work. What we can sign up for, what we know will give our life-long learners the skills they need as adults, and what will care for the kids that are sitting in front of us today.

The Mindful Practices' Model

Positive relationships with caring, emotionally available adults are critical for students' social emotional growth. These strong interpersonal relationships between learners and educators are fundamental to students' school experience, yet there are real obstacles—most often lack of time and compassion fatigue—that go unaddressed. It seems clear that many districts are waiting for educators to fix the problem themselves. Districts are providing crisis management and hoping that these problems will go away without examining the root cause: burned out teachers who lack time are not available, emotionally or practically, to form the human connections with students that help them thrive in school.

Mindful Practices' approach views the school experience as a balance between the intra- and interpersonal for both the student and the educator. As our founder, I stand behind Mindful Practices' work because it has been developed over a 15-year period in response to both student and educator needs. My team has worked in demographically and socio-economically diverse settings to develop and refine the activities contained within this book. We have been testing these SEL and wellness strategies in the field, with boots on the ground, since 2006.

I present this Mindful Practices model to you as a humble how-to guide for creating an impactful SEL school experience. I designed these tools to help educators and school leaders implement sustainable SEL and mindfulness practices with fidelity. However, before diving into the Mindful Practices approach outlined in this book, it must be said that it is incomplete. As my dear friend Dr. Kiljoong Kim advises practitioners, for this work to have the greatest impact, we need to pair educators with fields outside of education. We need to connect with pediatricians, trauma therapists, nutritionists, cultural experts, physical therapists, equity and inclusion specialists, community stakeholders—people who can help us, as educators, better understand the body's psychosomatic response to stress and how it impacts learning along with information that can make the material more culturally sensitive and responsive for the populations we are serving.

I hope you will find our Mindful Practices approach both helpful and practical. Besides its intentional emphasis on SEL and mindfulness, the prioritization of physical movement is one more component that makes this approach unique. I created these strategies and practical implementation tools to help develop your SEC and that of your students. I encourage you to envision how each of the ideas can be modified to meet the needs of the population you are serving. Utilize these strategies to build a sustainable SEL program for your classroom, but, more importantly, take time to create opportunities for student voice and agency so that the work is both relevant and meaningful.

As we move forward on this journey together, I urge you to pause and take a breath. Even though we are the adults in our classrooms, we are not perfect. Moreover, we do not need to be. We simply need to accept ourselves in the present and try our best to model Mindful Practices for our students each day. The school experience is the balance of SELF and SOCIAL, which includes our successful days and our challenging days. It is our job to teach our students the life skill of coping with stress and anxiety as much as it is our job to make sure they know a quadratic equation or the structure of a haiku poem. As I often say when coaching educators and administrators, it is important that we give ourselves permission not to be perfect. The most important thing is that we try our best.

> **A Note to Readers**: This book is gender neutral and uses they/them/their pronouns unless gender is specified by name and relationship. Please modify content and language based on the developmental needs of your student population.

1

An Approach, Not a Program

In my second year of teaching I had a student, Roger, who couldn't concentrate on my oh-so-fabulous poetry lesson because he was hungry. I didn't see that. I saw a student that was disrupting the lesson I worked all weekend creating. Each time he fidgeted or talked I thought, "Ugh, he doesn't appreciate the hard work that went into this lesson. He is disrupting all the students next to him! I worked WAY too hard on this lesson."

Finally, after trying to redirect multiple times, I disciplined him, as I did the next day *and* the day after that as his behavior continued. Venting to my colleagues in the faculty lounge later in the week about Roger (in a less-than-compassionate "I don't know what is wrong with this kid" type of way), I discovered that his younger sister, Brandy, had been caught sneaking food from the school cafeteria. Putting all the pieces together, we figured out that Roger was hungry. His younger siblings were hungry. Their mom was struggling with addiction, had not been home in two weeks, and they were unsure of where their next meal would come from. Of course, my poetry lesson didn't matter to him! He was stuck in the panic of meeting his and his siblings' basic needs with limited resources or support. This was coupled with concern for his mother's well-being along with hiding the truth so that they would not end up in foster care. Again. Reflecting on the structure of my classroom, I realized that there were no SEL or mindfulness tools to meet Roger's physical, emotional, or mental health needs. As an educator passionate about her craft, I naively thought that my dynamic lessons were enough to engage my students in learning, regardless of what was happening outside of the schoolhouse doors.

Witnessing many of my students struggle first-hand as an educator, I realized that I was failing them by only focusing on their academic needs. It was my responsibility to teach the whole child, not just the part that I thought should want to learn poetry. I needed to have an SEL-Informed Classroom where I was informed about, sensitive to and making time to practice Social Emotional Learning. An adaptive environment where my students' Intrapersonal (SELF) and Interpersonal (SOCIAL) needs could be in balance. Even though the best SEL or mindfulness strategies could not have put food in Roger's stomach or brought his mother home, they could have mitigated the crippling anxiety of the unknown. If my students were not given the tools to be ready to learn amid life's chaos, their ability to excel in school would be negatively impacted. By not creating space for my students' emotional needs within my classroom I unknowingly fueled the cycle of dysfunction and uncertainty in which many of them were enmeshed. If students did not walk out of my class at the end of the year with the SEL and mindfulness tools in place to succeed in life—alongside the ability to write a poem—then I didn't do my job. Especially at my school, which boasted "serving the whole child" and "creating life-long learners" in the mission statement emblazoned in the hallway my students walked every day on their way to my class.

For students to succeed in my classroom, I needed to create space in my instruction for learners to develop an awareness of their physical, emotional, and mental needs so that they would be empowered to move out of "survival mode" (fight, flight, or freeze) and be present and ready to learn.

What approach is going to best prepare my students to be self-aware and not only ready to learn but ready to build positive relationships with their peers, make healthy choices about their bodies, and tackle life with resiliency and determination? The best approaches are those that:

- frame the "why" behind the work for all adults, school stakeholders, students, and parents, without making it all about "improved" academic achievement
- create space for student voice and agency—*regularly!*—and check-in daily with students, in their own words (*not* teachers observing what they think a student may be thinking or feeling); ask them about their mood and energy; seek actionable insights, like if they need their seat moved or are too close to the door to concentrate
- support the well-being, self-care, and mental health needs of the adults and the students, shame-free, by promoting positive youth (and adult) identity
- provide clear answers to implementation questions for adults and students: Am I being graded on this? Am I being evaluated on this? How do I practice this at home? Who is expected to implement?

What time(s) am I expected to implement each day/week and for how many minutes total?
- build the SEC of all adult stakeholders in the school/district with hands-on, experiential training that honors their unique starting points with this work

So, What *Is* Social Emotional Learning?

CASEL's definition of Social Emotional Learning is the most widely known:

> The process through which all young people and adults acquire and apply the knowledge, skills, and attitudes to develop healthy identities, manage emotions and achieve personal and collective goals, feel and show empathy for others, establish and maintain supportive relationships, and make responsible and caring decisions.
>
> SEL advances educational equity and excellence through authentic school-family-community partnerships to establish learning environments and experiences that feature trusting and collaborative relationships, rigorous and meaningful curriculum and instruction, and ongoing evaluation. SEL can help address various forms of inequity and empower young people and adults to co-create thriving schools and contribute to safe, healthy, and just communities.
>
> (CASEL, 2020)

While this definition is very useful, it can feel cumbersome if we are new to the discipline. When working with educators across the country, I asked folx what SEL means to them, as boots-on-the-ground caring adults who teach or work with youth every day, they responded:

> SEL is a way to slow and calm the mind in order to be aware of our emotions and to be aware of what really matters so students (and adults!) can be happier, healthier people!
>
> SEL is learning about self and your relationships with others. Students can learn this by: connecting authentically with adults, by getting to know themselves and when I fuse SEL into academic content.
>
> SEL is an on-going process, a journey without end just as self-improvement is never ending. It's continuous building on previous growth. It's improving upon each improvement.
>
> As an educator, I use SEL in two ways: to build an interpersonal connection with my students before class starts (non-instructional time) AND to build my students awareness of their own emotions

to prevent frustration, stress and/or performance anxiety from negatively impacting their achievement.

SEL is the life-long process of understanding your emotions and how to manage them.

To me, SEL is an on-going, reciprocal process between students, peers, adults, staff, where everyone learns how to respond (rather than react) to stressful or disturbing situations, creating an atmosphere of safety and empathy.

As explored in these definitions, Figure 1.1 offers a visual representation of SEL emphasizing the balance between the Intrapersonal and the Interpersonal. The process of finding this balance is aligned with the 3 CASEL core competencies, Self-Awareness, Self-Management (or Self-Regulation) and Social Awareness, as well as to the development of Social Emotional Competence (SEC), each defined as:

> **Social and Emotional Competence (SEC)** is the capacity to coordinate cognition, affect, and behavior that allows individuals to thrive in diverse cultures and contexts and achieve specific tasks and positive developmental outcomes. . . . These clusters emphasize the importance of developing both intrapersonal competencies that include self-awareness and self-management and interpersonal competencies that include social awareness and relationship skills.
>
> **Self-Awareness**: The abilities to understand one's own emotions, thoughts, and values and how they influence behavior across contexts. This includes capacities to recognize one's strengths and limitations with a well-grounded sense of confidence and purpose.
>
> **Self-Management**: The abilities to manage one's emotions, thoughts, and behaviors effectively in different situations and to achieve goals and aspirations. This includes the capacities to delay gratification, manage stress, and feel motivation and agency to accomplish personal/collective goals.
>
> **Social Awareness**: The abilities to understand the perspectives of and empathize with others, including those from diverse backgrounds, cultures, and contexts. This includes the capacities to feel compassion for others, understand broader historical and social norms for behavior in different settings, and recognize family, school, and community resources and supports.
>
> (CASEL, 2020)

In these terms, the Mindful Practices SEL approach focuses on the following SEC clusters, with an added emphasis on the balance between Self-Efficacy

An Approach, Not a Program ◆ 13

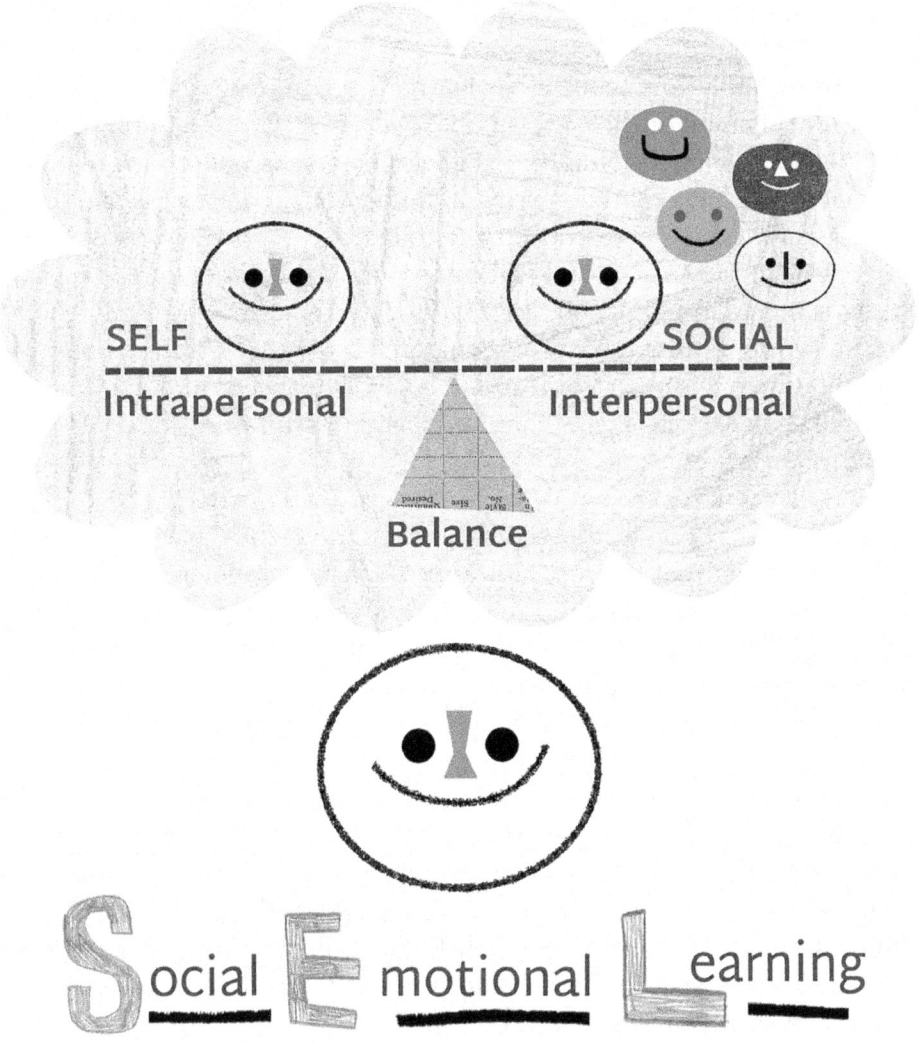

Figure 1.1 SEL: The Balance Between Intrapersonal and Interpersonal

and Social Harmony, as highlighted in the last few practices of both the SELF (Intrapersonal) and SOCIAL (Interpersonal) chapters, in activities such as the Community-Based Service Learning Project. When we working with schools and districts, we start with the simplified, learner-focused descriptions of the competencies below. We have found this helps keep the balance between the Intrapersonal and Interpersonal in focus. Also, we use the term Self-Regulation instead of Self-Management, as it resonates with students and adults alike.

Self-Awareness: Empowering the learner to address their mental, emotional, and physical needs.

Self-Regulation: Shifting the learner from impulsivity to intentional navigation of choices.

Social Awareness: Building the learner's awareness of self in social situations. What they bring into the room and how the overall energy and atmosphere impacts the collective.

Self-Efficacy and Social Harmony: When in balance, the learner feels centered, present, and like a valued and contributing member of the world around them. This competency also reflects the learner's ability to find their voice and to balance the needs of the self with the needs of others, without projection, assumption, or excessive self-sacrifice.

Mindfulness is one of the vehicles we use to create space for stillness. Space to cultivate that bedrock, intrapersonal SE competency, Self-Awareness. This book examines the interplay between interpersonal and intrapersonal SEL skill development and how the practices of vocalization, movement, stillness, and teamwork, or what we call *Mindful Practices* develop not only one's Self-Awareness but, in turn, an increased ability to connect with others.

Taking a cue from Precious Jennings' work at Columbia College in Chicago, "Self-Awareness is cultivated by the union between the body and mind found within these four practices: vocalization, movement, stillness and human connection." The goal of the POP Chart and the practices housed within is to build Self-Awareness, Self-Regulation, and Social Awareness so that students can balance the needs of the self with those of the collective, (Self-Efficacy and Social Harmony).

- **Vocalization**: speaking, chanting, singing
- **Movement**: gross/fine/locomotor, yoga, dance, fitness
- **Stillness**: reflection, breath work, meditation
- **Human Connection**: play, collaboration, communication

Each of these four practices is experiential in nature and will resonate differently with each student or adult, as folx all have different entry points to this work based upon myriad individual factors such as previous traumas or levels of physical mobility. To meet students and adults at that entry point, the practice is not merely reading about the positive impacts of breath work or movement on the body. Instead, it is paying attention on purpose (mindfulness)

An Approach, Not a Program ◆ 15

and, over time, cultivating an understanding of what one needs and when they need it (Self-Awareness).

With a POP Check (Figure 1.2) students (and/or adults) practice journaling, yoga, or breath work to meet the needs of their bodies and minds at that moment in time. Over time, this continual, intentional practice of cultivating Self-Awareness empowers adults and children alike to read and respond proactively to their bodies' cues instead of feeling victimized by their own emotional reactions or moments of dysregulation.

When adults and students have the Self-Awareness to read and respond proactively to their bodies' cues, they can act with agency, connect more authentically, form positive identities and engage in power sharing. One of the objectives of SEL integration across a school building must be adults engaging in intentional self-inquiry so that they can better witness and

Figure 1.2 The POP Check

reckon with their own SEC and how it impacts the climate and culture of their classrooms.

As discussed earlier, it is critical that time is allotted not only for educators to develop their SEC but to spend ample time evolving their own Self-Awareness, the bedrock of the Social Emotional competences. When educators develop their Self-Awareness, they better understand their own lenses and biases and have the tools to move beyond defining a student by a single story that they may or may not be reacting to in the present moment.

Development of educator Self-Awareness is critical for the anti-racist work that, together with well-being and SEL, must be inextricable from the fabric of how an SEL-informed classroom operates. For anti-racist work to be authentically implemented in schools, educators must encourage students to become agents of change, allowing for their voices and perspectives to be seen and heard. Educators and students act differently when they have agency and feel they can make a difference in the landscape of their school environment without sacrificing self-identity. They are able to build the relational trust needed to co-create and inform the climate and culture of a classroom, because they have the awareness to manage and understand their emotions, reactions, and needs and the energy they are bringing into the environment itself (Figure 1.3).

The word *practice* is intentionally used when framing the activities, as it is important that the work is messaged to adults and students alike as something they *practice*, instead of something they *master*. SEL should not seem or be performative, as it detracts from the authenticity of the experience and the learning that comes from practice. These Mindful Practices cultivate awareness of body and mind so that one can operate with compassion for self and others. Mindful Practices looks at the needs of the whole person—physical, emotional, and intellectual—and when these three are in balance, the student or adult is more able to learn.

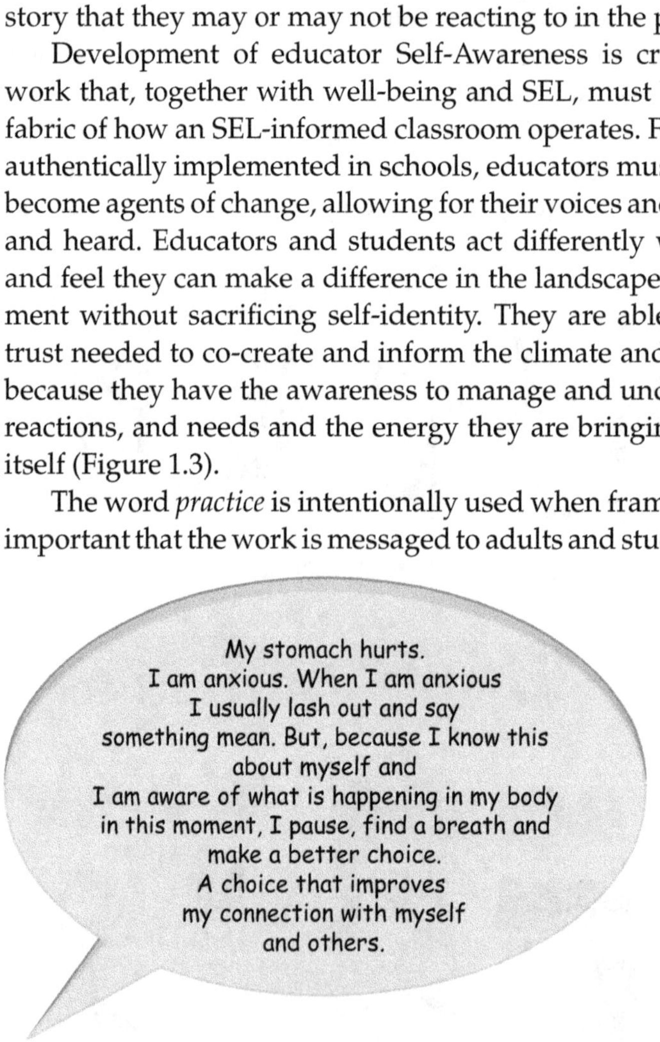

> My stomach hurts. I am anxious. When I am anxious I usually lash out and say something mean. But, because I know this about myself and I am aware of what is happening in my body in this moment, I pause, find a breath and make a better choice. A choice that improves my connection with myself and others.

Figure 1.3 Self-Awareness and Choice

Mindfulness is an important component of these practices; with its focus is on being *present*, or moving through distraction, to solve for the current moment in time, even if that solution is simply being still. Mindfulness empowers learners to, as Viktor Frankl said, find that space between stimulus and response, even when dysregulated. With its grace, simplicity, and ease, mindfulness creates the space in which adults and students can cultivate non-judgmental awareness of who they are and how who they are impacts their connections and interactions with others, encouraging the development of positive identity.

Non-judgmental awareness of who one is and what one needs is critical to students' socio-emotional well-being. Through this non-judgmental awareness of self, students create a positive youth identity—seeing that they have social emotional needs without viewing themselves as *broken*. The hope is that the awareness is cultivated within an environment that also prioritizes student agency. So, a student sees their emotional needs and has already experienced solutions that may meet those needs, hence the activities visibly posted in a POP Chart instead of being practiced and forgotten as a *one-off* activity.

What Is Mindfulness?

According to Mark Williams at the University of Oxford (Williams & Penman, 2011), "Mindfulness means non-judgmental awareness. A direct knowing of what is going on inside and outside of ourselves, moment by moment." Or, as Jon Kabat-Zinn (2002) simply states, "The awareness that emerges through paying attention on purpose."

Mindfulness practices give learners the tools to be present—be in the moment—without fear, shame, or judgment of self or others. Practicing mindfulness in schools gives students the tools to mitigate the factors that often negatively impact learning (hunger, fear, pain) so they are empowered to be present and ready to learn—about themselves, their peers, and your academic content.

Some practitioners do not include movement when teaching mindfulness. However, I view the inclusion of movement as a strengths-based, compassionate, and equitable approach to teaching mindfulness that cultivates positive youth identity by meeting students where they are in the moment and honoring that everyone has a different entry point to the practice (Figure 1.4).

As our Mindful Practices model illustrates, sometimes it is movement, not stillness, which is the most accessible and calming practice for

Table 1.1 Compare and Contrast: Mindfulness and Social Emotional Competencies

Mindfulness	Social Emotional Learning (SEL)
1. **Singularity**—focus on a single task at hand. The opposite of multitasking. Being fully present and engaged with one thing at a time. Space to cultivate body awareness.	1. **Self-Awareness**—identify how you are feeling and how it may be impacting your physical being. From passivity to acting with agency.
2. **Intentionality**—deliberate action moving past tendencies. The opposite of "responding on autopilot" or falling back into the same narrative. This requires disciplined habits of mind.	2. **Self-Regulation**—ability to respond from a place of calm knowing. Finding meaningful and resourceful ways to use your voice and own who you are and communicate what you need to those around you. From impulsivity to intentionally navigating choices.
3. **Non-Judgmentalness**—noticing yourself (thoughts, words, deeds) and the world around you without evaluation, judgment, assessment, or the need to label (actions, feelings, or emotions) *good* or *bad*.	3. **Social Awareness**—recognition that our words and actions impact our community, and ourselves. From a reactive, judgmental, or victimized mindset to a proactive, communal view of the world.
4. **Space**—The space to respond compassionately to different personal and social triggers without losing one's center or sacrificing social rapport. The opposite of dysfunctional *groupthink* or habitual, unconscious reactions to everyday events.	4. **Balance between Self-Efficacy and Social Harmony**—managing vulnerability with a compassionate understanding of one's relationship with SELF and with others. The needs of the SELF and the SOCIAL in balance create space for positive identity formation. From projection, assumption, or excessive self-sacrifice to feeling present, witnessed, and valued.

students—especially if those students have experienced trauma. Some students may not have experienced trauma but are negatively impacted by having too little sleep the night before or too much sugar at lunch earlier that afternoon. Or, they simply have different constitutions, just like adults. My husband likes to go to the gym to work off stress, while I like to curl up with *The New Yorker*. To "relax" on vacation, he wants to snowboard down the triple black bowl with our daredevil friends, while I want to gently glide down the green trail with a hot cocoa in one hand. Whether students or adults, what our bodies crave in states of stress or relaxation varies greatly. Therefore, a practitioner that is compassionate, flexible, and responsive, instead of looking for the quick and easy one-size-fits-all SEL model, will have a much more impactful approach.

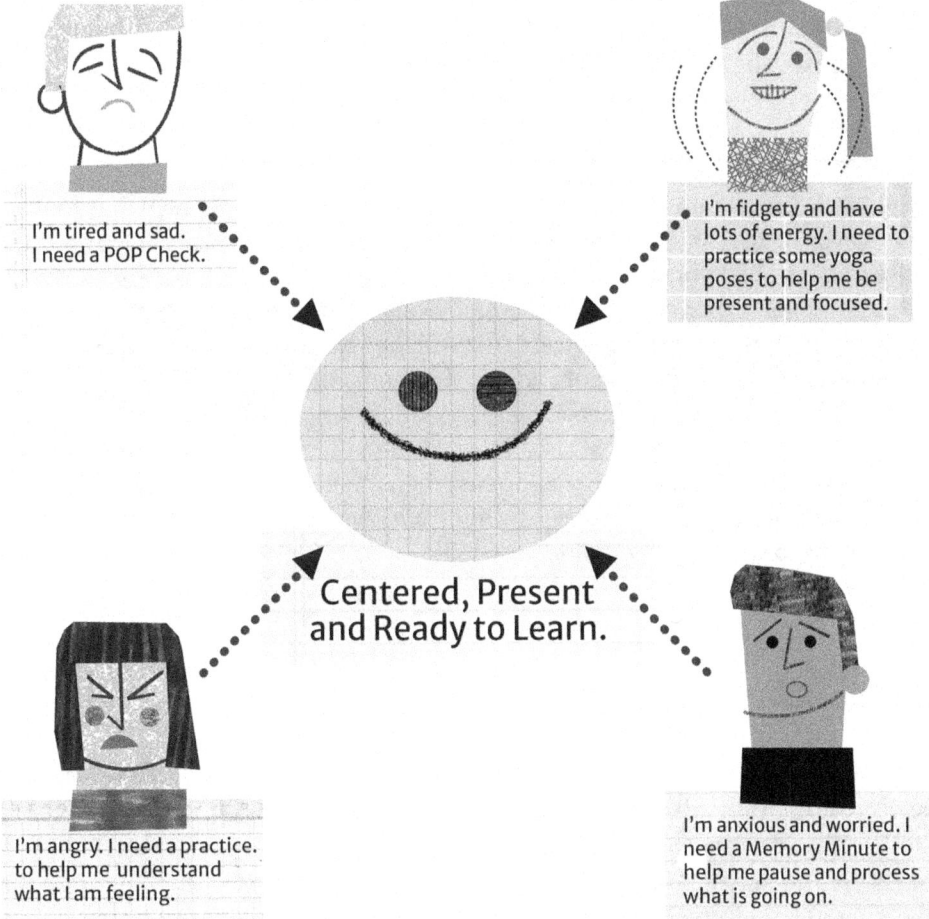

Figure 1.4 Different Ways to Get Back to Center

This variance in student need is why the SEL-informed classroom also includes movement, instead of only the standard seated and scripted approach. If the end goal is for students to be empowered with the tools to move through survival mode (fight, flight or freeze) when activated, then movement as well as stillness must be included for those learners that find movement more accessible and soothing. It is important that teachers meet students where they are and move their energy accordingly. As my dear friend Lara Veon, who is a trauma therapist and a member of my Mindful Practices team, articulates:

> Because each child's nervous system is unique, what is relaxing to one student might be activating to another. Stillness, for example, might actually activate the sympathetic nervous system—the stress response—instead of inducing a state of balance or relaxation. In these cases, movement with breath work can be helpful alternatives to bring the parasympathetic nervous system—the rest and relaxation response—back online for a child (Figure 1.4).

> **Educator Tip**: As Lara advises the educators she trains, it is imperative that adults endeavor to see all students and their behaviors through a culturally responsive and trauma-informed lens. We know trauma is a subjective nervous system reaction to an experience, not the actual event. When we understand the neurobiology of trauma and are aware that it might show up in the classroom, we can better create environments where students and teachers have the necessary tools for Self-Awareness and Self-Regulation. What is needed is an explanation of the neurobiology of trauma and how it manifests in student behavior. It requires us to understand what happens when the body is in a trauma response along with self-inquiry to critically examine our own cultural biases and standard responses to students' needs and actions.

Why Mindfulness for Educators?

When working with different schools across the country, I will occasionally see educators resort to using shaming language such as, "I don't know what is wrong with this class today. You all are acting like crazy people," in an attempt to corral a high-energy class. In confidence, those educators will often express that they "hated having to do that" but found themselves "at the end of their ropes." These dedicated teachers felt that they were out of strategies and emotional bandwidth to handle the situation in a way that reinforces, not dismantles, that human connection they are attempting to build with their students.

> The process of developing mindful habits is neurologically akin to developing physical skill sets that build muscle memory, like riding a bike or playing the guitar, and building cognitive schemas, like improving math skills or connecting narrative themes across literary genres. This is more than just an analogy because practicing acute and sustained awareness over time builds neural connections that fundamentally alter networks in the brain.... Improving mindfulness is important for teachers because it allows them to exert more effortful control over their own thoughts, emotions, and behaviors. Because negative thoughts can lead to distressing emotions, and because distressing emotions can lead to unproductive or disruptive behaviors, improving control in these domains can improve the chances that a teacher will make thoughtful and strategic choices when students are misbehaving or underperforming.

As my friend and co-author, Dr. Chris Soto, discusses earlier, mindfulness activities can help students and adults cultivate Self-Awareness to avoid retreating to a *fight, flight or freeze* response that shaming language or triggering situations often bring.

An SEL-Informed educator moves beyond merely implementing a program to a method of crafting instruction that meets the competing needs of the whole child. Looking at everything from a student's overall wellness (Is lack of sleep keeping a student from being present? Is a student's physical need to move their body keeping them from being able to focus?) to what drives student interactions (Is there a conflict with a peer that keeps a student's mind focused on *survival* instead of being present in the classroom?) We give educators the daily diagnostic tools to look beyond content delivery. When we frame the implementation of SEL and mindfulness in our classrooms around creating a community of learners that is empowered to be present, we are able to overcome the negative narrative (test scores, *problem students*, etc.) that often prevents educators from shedding biases, stepping into vulnerability, and building relational trust with students.

This book provides the tools needed for the implementation of an SEL and mindfulness approach that brings practitioner and student into a compassionate connection. We'll explore the belief that the goal of SEL and mindfulness—the ability to be present and aware in the moment to practice Self-Efficacy and contribute to Social Harmony—can be shared for both educator and student.

The Mindful Practices approach outlined in this book challenges school stakeholders to stop viewing SEL and mindfulness practices as something that *underperforming children* need as a *special program* and to understand this as a collective learning process needed by all, because everyone regularly experiences stress, anxiety, and unpleasant emotions. By shifting the emphasis from a handful of *problem children* receiving the services to SEL being a universal practice for the entire class, the Mindful Practices model outlined in this book will empower educators and students to cultivate SEL competencies through intentional practice in an accepting and shame-free classroom environment.

These practices provide educators and students with the tools to understand their connection to the world, how to positively express themselves within it, and how they can balance their own needs alongside the needs of the collective. When the school experience is reframed from the adult and child being in opposition to the collective working toward a common, interpersonal goal not only are life-long skills developed, but the school climate and culture also becomes physically, emotionally, and intellectually safer for all.

Name Expectations

In my work with schools across the country, I often find that the SEL competencies live in charts or posters on the walls but are rarely put to practical use. By creating a chart of observable behaviors, educators can make SEL more explicit and concrete, and teach what competencies *do* and *do not* look and sound like in your classroom. Let's take the guesswork out of SEL. We do not want our students to waste time and emotional energy decoding their teachers' idiosyncrasies in order to be successful.

I remember my first Christmas home with my boyfriend's (and now husband's) family. I wanted so badly to impress his mother and be a *good* houseguest. After dinner I made sure to clear the table. The next morning Rob told me that his mother thought I had done a sloppy job of loading the dishwasher because I put the silverware *in the wrong way*. (I grew up without a dishwasher and so I was not aware of the *knives down and forks up* rule.) I remember how irritated I was and I how judged I felt. I had tried my best and followed the rules, as I knew them, so how could his mother judge me so unfairly? How was I *supposed* to know? What was she saying about *my mom* and the way she raised me?

Often because we were raised a certain way, we expect that social skills are something our students *should* have or that the parents *should* be teaching them at home. We unfairly expect our students to have cultivated a social skill that they may have never been taught or that may look different from one culture to the next.

Begin with self-inquiry and examine the intentions behind your lesson. Your job is not to educate students on your cultural beliefs or social mores but rather to do the work of examining your own implicit biases. Reflect on how you can engage in vulnerable, authentic conversations with your students that build relational trust and foster human connection. Examine what you can own about your SEC process and how you can share your struggles, reflections, and observations to give them permission to do the same.

As many of us are guests in the communities in which we serve, it is our responsibility to reflect upon our sense of *right* (knives down in the dishwasher) and wrong (knives up in the dishwasher) and separate our own peccadilloes or desire for compliance from the social skills needed to succeed in life, such as active listening or respecting your neighbor's personal space. Take the time to learn about your students and share meaningful examples and observable behaviors so that they can step into Self-Awareness without shame and find their own voices around the SEL concepts. We must remember to approach this work compassionately and humbly, knowing that we will undoubtedly learn quite a lot about ourselves and the energy and expectations we bring into the room.

The Mindful Practices adaptive approach to SEL prioritizes the connection between student's awareness of their bodies and their ability to be present. "I only had a bag of Skittles for breakfast and I am having a difficult time concentrating." Or, "I know I am anxious because my palms are sweating and my head aches." Educators using our approach make time for students to practice Self-Awareness and give them space to make informed decisions about their behavior when they are dysregulated.

Students or adults who are dysregulated may complain of physical symptoms (often with a psychosomatic cause) such as chest pain, fatigue, dizziness, migraine/headache, back pain, shortness of breath, abdominal pain, insomnia, and numbness. Trauma Therapist Lara Veon often refers to this process as *somatization*, or when students are experiencing psychological distress in the form of physical symptoms.

We have a responsibility to examine our biases and cannot jump to the conclusion that a student's physical symptoms only have a psychological cause (as there may be a physical cause that needs immediate attention). Instead, let's move toward a model of embodied teaching and invite the student to observe what is happening in his body and mind. See this as an opportunity to employ the mindfulness practice of noticing or witnessing one's experience in the moment without judgment (scripted material is *in italic type* throughout the book); for example: *Luke, I hear you say that you often have a headache before we practice writing. Do you feel that is what is happening in your body? Would you like to chat about what to do next time we are writing and you feel your head starting to hurt?*

Just as a student must learn to add before they can subtract, we can't expect a student to regulate a behavior if they are unaware of its source. The balance between Self-Efficacy and Social Harmony (or, the duality between the intrapersonal and the interpersonal) is achieved when teachers and students build competence by working through the stages of Self-Awareness, Self-Regulation, and Social Awareness. Our model places Self-Awareness as the precursor to Self-Regulation, as we must be aware of a behavior in order to regulate it. That being said, because the contexts in which we live our lives are constantly shifting, the journey of the self progressing from basic needs onward is hardly linear. The emphasis here is on the balance between the *intrapersonal* and *interpersonal*, as school necessitates that learners balance the needs of the individual ("I want to get an A on this worksheet!") with the challenges of the collective ("But I can't concentrate because Sarita keeps talking, which is giving me a headache. I want to punch her, but know I can't or I will end up in the principal's office. But, the teacher isn't doing anything about it because he is too busy helping another student who is still stuck on problem number 4"). School is an intrapersonal pursuit housed within an interpersonal construct. To be an effective student, learners must astutely juggle both sets of needs.

Progress monitoring of SEL competencies, the same way we would for academic content, is key. However, because students' contexts are constantly shifting and changing, I caution us from looking at mastery of SEL competencies as the primary outcome. For the past seven years, my research partner, Dr. Kiljoong Kim at Chapin Hall at the University of Chicago, has studied the impact of the Mindful Practices model on both adult and student SEL skill development, as well as the importance of student voice and agency in this process. In his research he found that:

> Similar to mathematics, a student can perform computation when presented as is, but is unable to perform that same computation in a word problem. That is, one can display mastery of Self-Awareness but may not be able to apply that same Self-Awareness in different contexts. This doesn't mean that measuring mastery is useless, it means that Self-Awareness needs to be explored in varying contexts (among friends, during a test, outside of school, etc.) and, when possible, expressed in the learner's own words. (Instead of an adult trying to guess what a student is feeling or expressing.) Knowing the level

Table 1.2 Sample Charts: Observable SEL Behavior

Self-Awareness: Body Awareness	
Does look like sound like	**Does NOT** look like sound like
• Practicing safe touch • Respecting your neighbor's personal space No means NO • Using your voice when someone is making you feel uncomfortable • Acting with agency and making healthy lifestyle choices (eating nutritional whole foods, drinking water, getting enough sleep, etc.)	• Touching someone's hair, body, etc. without permission • Touching someone sexually, violently, or in a way that is not appropriate for school • Physical intimidation • Laughing at or dismissing someone who requests personal space • Commenting on someone's clothes or appearance • Making unhealthy lifestyle choices (junk food, excessive caffeine or refined sugar, drugs, alcohol, sleep deprivation, etc.)
Self-Regulation: Expressing Emotions and Managing Stress, Anger, and Anxiety	
Does look like sound like	**Does NOT** look like sound like
• Utilizing our POP Chart as you enter class to honor where you are each day • Respecting our Agreements • Practicing mindfulness, movement, or breath work practices to manage unpleasant emotions • Using our Talking Stick to create a space to discuss difficult topics • Finding your voice • Honoring your well-being needs so that you can be present and ready to learn	• Eye-rolling, grunting, or making comments under your breath • Breaking our Agreements • Dismissing your or others' pain, anger, or emotions • Abusing yourself, others, or substances to manage unpleasant emotions • Dishonoring our compassionate space

Table 1.2 (Continued)

Social Awareness: Active Listening and Service Orientation	
Does look like sound like	**Does NOT** look like sound like
• Respecting others' feelings, emotions, races, cultures, age, sexual orientation, and opinions so that all voices can be heard • Using our communication tools to honor voice and agency • Honoring our compassionate classroom • Honoring learners with exceptionalities • Honoring English Language Learners	• Focusing our attention on distractions like phones or food • Laughing at others' feelings, emotions, opinions, or language/accent • Making negative comments like "that's stupid" or "what a dumb idea!" • Dominating the group with your voice • Speaking negatively or making assumptions about others' races, ethnicities, cultures, religions, sexual orientation, gender, etc.
Self-Efficacy and Social Harmony: Balance between Intrapersonal and Interpersonal	
Does look like sound like	**Does NOT** look like sound like
• Leadership • Managing vulnerability • Human connection • Being present and operating with compassion toward self and others • Prioritizing well-being • Positive youth identity • Using our communication tools • Being culturally sensitive and examining implicit bias • Finding voice • Acting with agency	• Eye-rolling, grunting, or making comments under our breath • Breaking the Agreements • Focusing our attention on distractions like phones or food • Laughing at others' feelings, emotions, or opinions • Making negative comments like "That's stupid" or "What a dumb idea!" • Dominating the group with our voice • Speaking negatively or making assumptions about others' races, ethnicities, cultures, religions, sexual orientation, gender, etc. • Dishonoring our compassionate classroom

Note: Please modify chart for the grade level you teach.

of mastery of SE competency is helpful in that it can often tell you whether that student is ready to expand their level of exposure, or not.

Therefore, instead of mastery as the primary end goal, the goal of progress monitoring becomes agency—to give the learner (whether an adult or child) an increased awareness of their own skill development via practice over time.

As CASEL highlights, SEL practices that are implemented with fidelity should emphasize both positive youth identity and school connectedness. Which means looking not only at Adult SEC but also ensuring that SEL implementation consists of practices for the whole class, not just for a few *problem students*.

All students and educators experience stress that keeps them from being present in the classroom; therefore, both students and educators need to practice SEL and mindfulness with the same intentionality as core content. By pre-teaching concepts, scaffolding material and progress monitoring to assess need, educators can not only implement with fidelity but can also involve students in shaping the way that SEL is taught and practiced. Instead of SEL happening *to* students, adults are practicing SEL *with* students. As discussed earlier, if educators claim that life-long learning is their priority, then cultivating student voice and agency should be the driver of SEL implementation.

Districts in which school connectedness is a priority make time for educators to intentionally connect with students and build relational trust. In turn, when relational trust is built, students have more opportunities to use their voices—and educators are more open to listen. This compassionate, judgment-free listening creates opportunities for students to not only develop a positive self-identify but also for educators to create space for students to act with agency and co-create their learning experience.

School, when agency is a priority, can become a more equitable and culturally responsive place where students are given voice and choice. Where students see that how they feel about their experience as learners *matters*.

> **Native and Indigenous Students and SEL**
>
> Students within reservation schools and those in mainstream settings are highly capable, creative, innovative, and passionate. Their multidimensional attributes are of marvelous abundance! They prosper when teachers engage learning within their hearts as with learning in their minds. Given a collective staff commitment focused on academic

proficiency and strategically scaffolded by holistic wellness, every student will grow as an *autonomous learner*. An autonomous learner is one who is also *sovereign*. That is, they are entrusted to guide and cultivate their own learning in collaboration with peers, teachers, parents, elders, extended family, and community members.

Several critical components must be in place to support the sovereign learner, beginning with the intentional integration of Indigenous concepts. These concepts (ways of knowing and doing) must be championed by Native and Indigenous leaders; the ones whose lives are a testimony to the value of heritage, culture, and language. Second, Native and Indigenous mentor support is critical in negotiating school culture, much of which is driven by a dominant worldview. Third, parents, extended family, and Native and Indigenous community members are catalysts for needed essential sanctioning regarding negotiating dominant culture and these linear systems that drive a place called *school*.

There is much visibility and focus on SE competencies and the resulting increase in student wellness and academic proficiency. To the critical question, "Is there a complementary spectrum of SEL that can be re-envisioned through the rich lens of our First Nations' Peoples?" the resounding answer is "Yes"! It is incumbent upon us, as educators who have Indigenous students in our learning environments, to seek out Indigenous voices in this re-envisioning process. These authentic voices can navigate the two complex worlds that Native students exist within; that of Indigenous and Eurocentric. Lastly, given the vastly changing ethnic texture of our students, our SEL approaches must be undergirded by a central framework with a scaffolding of culture and equity. In other words, all SEL must be equitable and culturally driven as well as sustainable. As our country's racial demographics are shifting, educators must powerfully engage in courageous conversations and take bold actions to obliterate the vast inequities that are present within the schools that our black and brown students grace.

Dr. Elizabeth Johnson, Eastern Michigan University

2

Three Steps for Getting Started

Many educators ask me, "How do I get started?" Outlined in the pages of this chapter are three steps for moving forward with an intentional and adaptive approach for your SEL-informed classroom.

1. Begin With Adults, Specifically Well-Being

Whether you are beginning the SEL journey or widening your practice, pause and take a moment to assess your own SE competency or what Jennings and Greenberg called in their 2009 piece, *The Prosocial Classroom*, Social Emotional Competence (SEC). Intuitively we know that educators cannot teach what they cannot model, but if we are asking you to build human connections with students we must also make sure you are emotionally available to do so.

The goal of professional learning in SEL and mindfulness is to empower school stakeholders (including paraprofessionals and all support staff) with the capacity to apply appropriate SEL strategies based on context and need. The first step in developing Adult SE competence is creating space for stakeholder well-being so that all caring adults in a school system feel comfortable stepping into the vulnerability of speaking and addressing their mental and emotional needs to avoid the burnout, hypertension, and compassion fatigue that often comes with navigating our increasingly complex educational system.

Working with youth is very hard work, and I have found that educators are, by default, nurturers who will run their tanks on empty before thinking to take a moment for themselves. So, what does well-being look like in practice?

Time is our greatest commodity. Ask your administrators to re-designate existing professional learning time for well-being work. Not a separate, after-school well-being class where folx either feel guilty for going ("I need to spend time with my kids, I haven't seen them all day. And, if I ask the babysitter to stay late it will cost me an extra $25"), or guilty for not going ("I should take care of myself for a change, I am always taking care of others").

When looking at our own SEC, the Flip/Flop Observation and Coaching Log (Table 2.1) and the Social Emotional Learning Teacher Reflection Tool (Table 2.2) in this chapter are excellent ways for us, as educators, to reflect on our practice, assess need, and fill in the gaps. If you are trying this alone in your school as an innovator, or you are one in a cohort of many, these tools empower you to take the time to reflect on what is working and what is not so that you can approach both your and your students' SEL needs from a contemplative place.

When running on fumes becomes the daily routine, that routine becomes comfortable, and stepping outside of it is uncomfortable, even if it is healthier. Additionally, if our school culture rewards *busy* over *well-being* it is difficult for us to step into self-care if shame and judgment cloud our vision. What if we shifted the conversation? If we want time to practice and model well-being we need our school culture to prioritize these practices and honor their value. We are human. We get frustrated and frazzled throughout the school day and fall victim to quick fixes. We need support. SEL and mindfulness instruction will be more impactful when the work is rooted in empowering all students and educators with the well-being tools to take care of their needs.

Development of our well-being and SEC, as educators, is the necessary precursor to cultivating the SE competency of our students. As educators, we are the delivery vehicles by which the information is conveyed. The practices start with us. Educator SEC cannot be automatically assumed, the same way we wouldn't assume that all educators in the United States are proficient in teaching language arts simply because they live in an English-speaking country.

If the Department of Education adopted violin standards requiring each and every educator to deliver proficient violin instruction, there would be outrage. Administrators across the country would decry that we have not trained our educators to deliver violin instruction appropriately. They would fear that lack of educator knowledge would lead to unsatisfactory teaching and the spreading of misinformation about the violin. There would be concern that suggesting that anyone can teach violin without proper training

Table 2.1 Flip/Flop Observation and Coaching Log

Name of Observer: **Date:**
Name of Educator and School: **Time of Day:**
Room Number and Duration of Observation:

What the Educator Is Saying/Doing *(Intentional focus on educator SEL language and supports)*				What the Students Are Saying/Doing		

SEL Competency and Focus (Descriptors)

Self-Awareness	Self-Regulation	Social Awareness	Self-Efficacy + Social Harmony
Self-esteem, body awareness, personal responsibility, emotional awareness, understanding choice	Adaptability, expressing emotions, managing stress and anxiety, problem-solving, coping skills, decision-making skills	Active listening, empathy, service orientation, community-building, self-inquiry (self with others)	Compassion, relationships, voice, positive youth identity leadership, managing vulnerability, collaboration, teamwork, agency

SEL Tools/Practices

☐ POP Chart	☐ Movement ☐ Yoga ☐ Dance ☐ Vocalization	☐ Reflection
☐ Pair/group work	☐ Breath work ☐ Mindfulness ☐ Stillness	☐ Mindfulness
☐ Connection	☐ Other	☐ Other

Three Steps for Getting Started ◆ 31

would devalue the content and its delivery. And all these concerns would undoubtedly be valid.

This begs the question: if we would never think to adopt violin standards in this way, why did we do it with SEL? We must move schools beyond simply purchasing a pre-fab program that does not address well-being or SEC. If we agree that we would never just hand an educator a violin and expect them to be able to teach it proficiently, SEL must be viewed the same way.

State standards for SEL *are* a big step in the right direction as they move SEL from the realm of suggested content to a core competency vital to a student's academic success. The important next step is to look at the implementation side of the standards. How can we develop our competence in a way that meets our well-being needs both as people and educators?

I have found that the educators who are most successful implementing these practices are those who begin with the bedrock SE competency, Self-Awareness. They spend months cultivating their awareness of self and are compassionate with themselves along the way. These practitioners embrace the split vision between educator and learner and view the experiential learning process as the reflective springboard for not only effectively teaching SEL but for personal growth as well.

The tools featured in the pages that follow are to assist with that reflective process. They are *not* designed to be used for evaluation by an administrator but rather for self-exploration and/or engaging in conversations with a compassionate and non-judgmental thought partner.

2. Balance Management With Awareness

By giving students and educators a compassionate space to name their well-being and emotional needs we not only begin to omit the judgment and shame associated with the process, we also equip them with the tools to step into vulnerability and address their needs. I encourage educators to participate in the POP Check daily to model this practice for their students. It is powerful for students to witness their teachers practicing self-care in an open and transparent way, and it is also the perfect opportunity for educators to address their well-being needs in real time.

Good teaching is subject to compassion. Whether we are working with a student to tame their crippling fear of failure or if we are struggling to keep our cool when a challenging student pushes our buttons, our level of compassion toward our students can often be predicted by our level of compassion *toward ourselves*. Educators must model compassion toward themselves and

Table 2.2 Social Emotional Learning Educator Reflection Tool

What does SEL look like, sound like, and feel like in my classroom?

This document is to be used as a reflection tool or to be shared with a thought partner conducting informal observations. This tool is meant to help sculpt an SEL approach for students with challenging behaviors or chronic whole-class, behavioral issues. This is a reflection tool and is *not* to be tied to an educator's formal observation, unless explicitly stated by an administrator *before* the process has begun.

Please modify chart for the grade level you teach.

Educator Name: Name of Student Observed:

Was whole-class behavior observed? (Circle one) Yes No

Record each date in a different colored pen/pencil/marker for ease of reference.

Date One: Date Two: Date Three:

Student Observable Behavior	Observable Educator Response to Student	Educator Physical, Emotional, and Mental Experience	Educator Well-Being Practices
☐☐☐☐ lethargy/sleepy ☐☐☐☐ low tone ☐☐☐☐ refusal to participate ☐☐☐☐ attention seeking ☐☐☐☐ impulsive ☐☐☐☐ talks out of turn ☐☐☐☐ cannot stay in seat ☐☐☐☐ frenetic	☐☐☐☐ ignores behavior ☐☐☐☐ addresses issue as whole-class problem ☐☐☐☐ lower expectations for student ☐☐☐☐ higher expectations for student ☐☐☐☐ positive reinforcement	☐☐☐☐ lethargy/sleepy ☐☐☐☐ compassion fatigue ☐☐☐☐ overwhelmed ☐☐☐☐ frustrated ☐☐☐☐ address issue as whole-school problem ☐☐☐☐ addresses issue as parent problem	☐☐☐☐ **Physical**: day/time/duration: Outcome: ☐☐☐☐ **Mental**: day/time/duration: Outcome:

(Continued)

Table 2.2 (Continued)

Student Observable Behavior	Observable Educator Response to Student	Educator Physical, Emotional, and Mental Experience	Educator Well-Being Practices
☐☐☐☐ easily triggered/combative ☐☐☐☐ nosy/tattling/intrusive ☐☐☐☐ perfectionist ☐☐☐☐ lacks motivation to learn ☐☐☐☐ bossy ☐☐☐☐ defiant ☐☐☐☐ constantly complaining ☐☐☐☐ chronically unprepared for class ☐☐☐☐ easily distracted ☐☐☐☐ feels ignored/neglected/others favored ☐☐☐☐ fidgety ☐☐☐☐ chronically unclean ☐☐☐☐ no boundaries/personal space ☐☐☐☐ bullies others ☐☐☐☐ victim of bullying	☐☐☐☐ punitive measures ☐☐☐☐ threatens to take away privilege ☐☐☐☐ takes away privilege ☐☐☐☐ sends student out of room ☐☐☐☐ use token economy/PBIS ☐☐☐☐ give student time out ☐☐☐☐ promotes positive youth identity ☐☐☐☐ yell/raise voice ☐☐☐☐ shame/scream ☐☐☐☐ non-verbal cues (flash lights, proximity) ☐☐☐☐ plays favorites ☐☐☐☐ positive side bar with student to promote agency: "You can do it!" ☐☐☐☐ corrective side bar with student: "I am SO disappointed in you."	☐☐☐☐ hyper vigilance ☐☐☐☐ perfectionist ☐☐☐☐ sense of urgency ☐☐☐☐ anxiety ☐☐☐☐ helpless/powerless ☐☐☐☐ lacks motivation/given up on certain kids ☐☐☐☐ consistently overwhelmed by positive emotions ☐☐☐☐ consistently overwhelmed by negative emotions ☐☐☐☐ negative Nelly/downer ☐☐☐☐ shame ☐☐☐☐ easily triggered/combative ☐☐☐☐ feels ignored/neglected/others favored ☐☐☐☐ chronically unprepared/missing deadlines	☐☐☐☐ **Emotional:** Day/Time/Duration: Outcome: ☐☐☐☐ **Other (i.e., Collegial, etc.):** Day/Time/Duration: Outcome:

☐☐☐☐ consistently overwhelmed by positive emotions/excitement	☐☐☐☐ movement break: whole class ☐☐☐☐ movement break: individual student ☐☐☐☐ promotes student voice ☐☐☐☐ other	☐☐☐☐ defiant ☐☐☐☐ not collegial/collaborative ☐☐☐☐ other	
Classroom SEL Artifacts	**SEL Competencies Explicitly Taught**	**SEL Teaching Methodology**	**SEL Language Observed** *Record examples of explicit SEL cueing, redirecting, student conversations, etc.*
☐☐☐☐ Agreements ☐☐☐☐ daily schedule (including SEL and standards) ☐☐☐☐ student SEL stories or SEL artifacts on display ☐☐☐☐ Talking Stick ☐☐☐☐ Movement or Cool Down Corner ☐☐☐☐ POP Chart ☐☐☐☐ Other	☐☐☐☐ **Self-Awareness** day/time/duration: Practice: ☐☐☐☐ **Self-Regulation** day/time/duration: Practice: ☐☐☐☐ **Social Awareness** day/time/duration: Practice: ☐☐☐☐ **Self-Efficacy and Social Harmony** day/time/duration: Practice:	☐☐☐☐ **Vocalization** day/time/duration: Student Response: ☐☐☐☐ **Movement** day/time/duration: Student Response: ☐☐☐☐ **Stillness** day/time/duration: Student Response: ☐☐☐☐ **Connection** day/time/duration: Student Response:	"I see students demonstrating Self-Awareness and Self-Regulation skills by honoring their neighbor's personal space while working in small groups." "Students, what do we need to do right now to be ready to learn?"

their students. An educator's ability to be compassionate—toward themselves and their students—is something that is felt immediately upon entering their room. It is a space where students feel seen with a compassionate lens. Negativity toward one student is often sensed by the rest of the class and erodes the climate and culture of the classroom. One student being unwelcome in a room does not make the others feel inherently *more* welcome. A classroom that welcomes all, even those that test our patience, creates a consistent, emotionally resilient, and compassionate environment for learning—or, as Charlotte Danielson describes, an "environment of respect and rapport" (2011) in which students will feel they have the space to explore Self-Awareness without shame.

School is equally a personal and interpersonal pursuit. To be successful, our students must learn to balance the needs of the self with the needs of the collective. The secret here is to explicitly teach the competencies without becoming the domineering narrator inside your students' heads. As a former teacher, I knew many educators whose style was so militant and prescriptive that there was no room for student Self-Awareness to be cultivated. Students never learn to be self-aware or to self-regulate, they simply learn to comply.

By explicitly teaching SEL to students we are empowering them with the knowledge of what can work for them as learners. Often, educators and administrators are having these conversations behind the scenes: "Let's put Lina in Ms. Nicole's room next year, because she is a go-getter who does a lot of cooperative learning and Lina is a kinesthetic learner who has a lot of energy." By sharing this behind-the-scenes logic with both students and their parents, they are empowered with the knowledge of what kind of learning environment is needed for success. I often witness schools making informed decisions about a student's learning environment but not sharing the "Why" behind these decisions with the students or families themselves.

When the student leaves a school (and the community that knows their SEL needs) and moves on to the new environment (where their SEL needs are unknown), they often face challenges. A student might know that they "liked the way that their old teacher taught," but they are not empowered with the Self-Awareness or the words to voice their needs as new environments present themselves. Transparency and opportunities to use their voices are key for students to take ownership of the SEL process find agency as learners. As John Hattie notes in *Visible Learning* (2009), educators modeling and discussing SEL strategies in real time is one of the most impactful implementation methods, as it promotes student agency and ownership. Hattie also notes that social skill training should be provided "on a regular and sustained basis" and found that training was most effective "when interventions lasted for 40 lessons or more." Additionally, measured, predictable, and consistent delivery must take place over time, as Catherine Cook-Cottone's work (2015) around "dosage" demonstrates. This is why checking in daily with the POP Chart becomes a daily component of a classroom routine. Instead of reacting to student behavior or merely managing a class, a teacher facilitates shame-free opportunities for students to cultivate Self-Awareness, voice, and agency promoting positive youth identity, even in growth areas.

By defining what is *managing* your students' behavior (i.e. classroom management, classroom consequences, etc.) and what is SEL (i.e. giving students the space and agency to develop their own Self-Awareness and Self-Regulation skills so that they can *manage* their own behavior), educators create a clearly defined set of expectations and routines. An educator approaches student issues consistently and predictably from the vantage point of an ally wanting to assist in the growth of their Self-Awareness. The SEL-informed educator sets clear and consistent expectations. And, instead of being emotionally reactive or shaming when those expectations are not met, has the Self-Awareness to realize that they may be triggered, pauses to take a breath, and works with the student to seek prevention out of awareness.

For instance, let's say a student enters your class and loudly throws their backpack. In years past, our conversation with that student might have sounded something like this:

Teacher: Sarah! How dare you throw your backpack around! You need to have more respect for your things and the people around you. I don't know what is allowed at home, but that type of baby behavior is not welcome in my class. Next time you come in here and disrupt my class I am sending you down to the principal's office.
Sarah: Yeah. OK.
Teacher: Look at me when I am speaking to you, Sarah. Do you understand me?
Sarah: Yes.

Now, the conversation most likely sounds something like:

Teacher: What is going on, Sarah? Why did you throw your backpack? You are being loud and disruptive.
Sarah: Renata and Dorothy were just mean to me for no reason. I hate school! Everyone is mean!
Teacher: OK, well, I know that you are feeling angry and frustrated, but it is not appropriate for you to throw your backpack.
Sarah: [Student looks away.] Yeah. OK. I won't do it again. Sorry.

As educators, we have an almost preternatural inclination to protect our instructional time. In this case, Sarah disrupts our class, which eats away at our instructional minutes. We don't want this to happen again, so we discuss backpack-throwing with Sarah and feel our job is done. We protect the flow of our day, and we raise the students' awareness about a problematic behavior so it doesn't happen again. In this scenario, the teacher also tells Sarah *what* she is feeling instead of giving her the space to cultivate awareness, speak her needs, and find her voice. This is not SEL, as it does not build the student's Self-Awareness, it only benefits the teacher so the problem behavior won't continue and they can move forward.

An SEL-informed conversation would sound something like this:

Teacher: Sarah, I noticed that you threw your backpack. Take a moment to pause and find your breath. [Teacher pauses to take a breath, modeling for the student. Student takes a breath.] Would you like to share what is going on?

Sarah: No. [pause] I am not ready yet.

Teacher: OK. Take your time. Would you like to visit the POP Chart and then we will talk?

Sarah: Sure.

Teacher: Great. Please come see me when you are done. Thank you.

[Student goes to POP Chart for 3 minutes. Then walks over to teacher.]

Sarah: Renata and Dorothy were just mean to me for no reason.

Teacher: OK, so why did you throw your backpack?

Sarah: Um. I dunno.

Teacher: Can you own what you are feeling? Can you tell me about your emotions?

Sarah: Angry and mad.

Teacher: It is OK to feel angry and mad. But it is not OK to throw objects in our classroom that may hurt yourself or others. So, next time you are angry or frustrated what can you practice? What activities from our POP Chart do you like to practice?

Sarah: I like Memory Minute and the yoga poses.

Teacher: OK, so how about next time you are angry you take a moment to sit down and practice a Memory Minute? Will that work?

Sarah: Yes. I think so. I can try it. And I am sorry about backpack.

Teacher: Thank you for apologizing. Now we both know what caused you to throw your backpack, which is a positive step toward building Self-Awareness. The most important thing is that you are empowered with a solution next time you are upset.

Three Steps for Getting Started ◆ 39

Sarah: Yes. Thanks, Mr. Jakubowski.

Teacher: Anytime, Sarah. Talking about how we are feeling and finding practices that help us make positive choices about our behavior is what Social Emotional Learning is all about.

In this final scenario, the teacher creates space for Sarah to build Self-Awareness and give voice to her feelings. This is SEL, as it builds the student's Self-Awareness, and gives her the mindfulness and life-long learning tools to PAUSE take a breath—OWN what is happening—and PRACTICE an informed choice. By intentionally shifting the focus from "disciplining" students to creating self-reliant learners who are able to regulate their own emotional responses, students have agency to be the solution and own their educational experience.

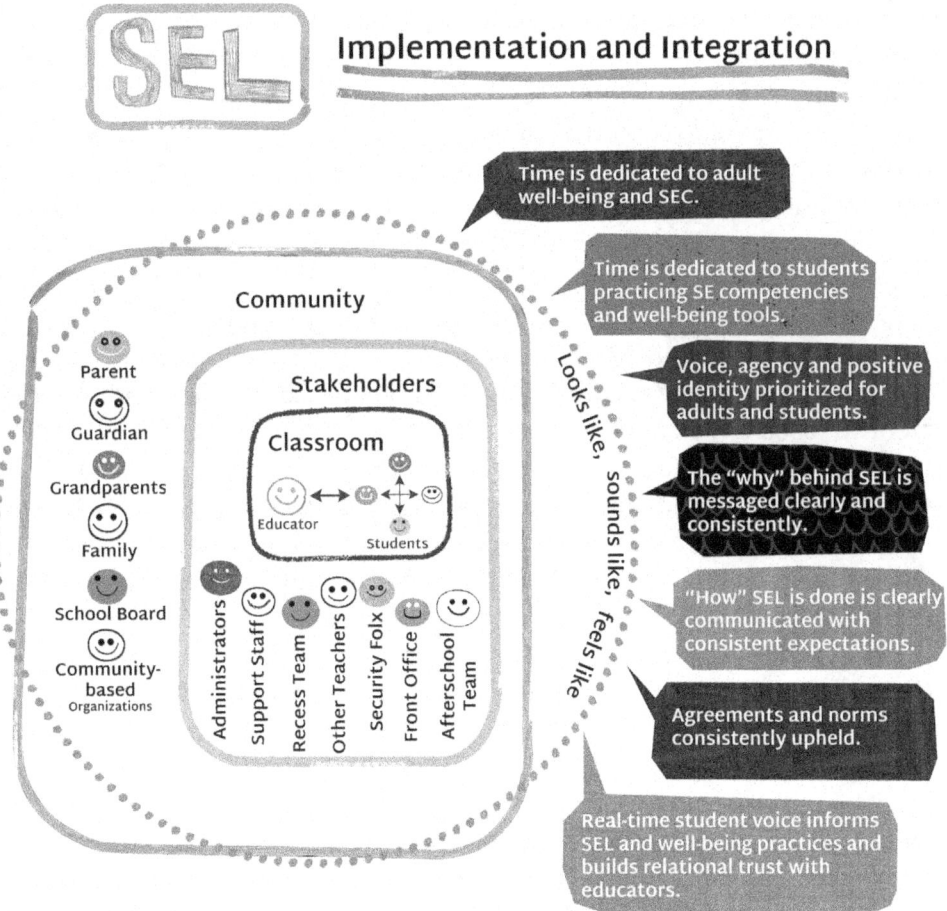

Figure 2.1 SEL Implementation and Integration

3. Model Well-Being Practices

As educators we don't have favorite students. But, I remember one, Javier or "Javie," that still lives in my heart. He was a "glue kid"; the type that brought other kids together. He was friends with everyone and made everyone comfortable around him.

Javie had a rough time at home. His house was a chaotic place, and he often came to school hungry and having slept in his clothes. From conversations with the school social worker I knew Javie had witnessed physical abuse toward his mother from her off-and-on-again alcoholic partner. There was little quiet or routine in Javie's life, so sitting still and working within a structured environment were two competencies with which he consistently struggled.

Even with all the challenges he faced, Javie was the light of our class. He excelled at group work, or any sort of collaborate-with-your-peers project. But, the sense of humor and gregarious personality that helped Javie thrive in a group setting also made him struggle during classroom activities that required stillness, like silent work.

It never failed; the minute I finally got the class to be quiet, Javie talked out of turn, sent a paper ball flying across the room, or interrupted our lesson with a non-instructional question like, "Why is our mascot a lynx? Nobody even knows what a lynx is. That is stupid!" Exasperated I would turn to him with pleading eyes and say, "Javie, why did you just do that? We just talked about talking out of turn *yesterday*!" He would invariably look up at me, smile, and say, "I dunno, Ms. T. I'm sorry."

Was he lying to me? Did he know *why* it was uncomfortable for him to sit still or to focus or be comfortable in quiet? No. In the chaos of Javie's life or in his schooling thus far, he had never been given the time or space to learn what triggered him and how to appropriately respond. He had never had the opportunity to cultivate Self-Awareness; he was often simply disciplined or taken to the principal's office. He told me that he regularly felt out of control or powerless, as his actions seemed to control him.

I knew that Javie was coping with stress and impulse control, but as a new teacher without SEL or mindfulness tools in my toolbox yet, I often felt ineffective in coaching him how to be the student I needed him to be to succeed in my class. Some students may be dealing with the pain of living in poverty, some may be dealing with the stressors of a fiercely competitive academic environment, and others, like Javie and Roger, may be coping with a tough home life that negatively impacts their ability to focus on the present moment and learn.

Harking back to Roger's story at the beginning of this book, there are multiple reasons to connect well-being and SEL practices in schools. We want students to operate with agency and make the connection (Self-Awareness) between what they put into their bodies and how their bodies and minds function. How do their choices, when choice is available, around sleeping, eating, drinking, stress, and exercise impact them as learners?

An additional layer to the wellness piece is being aware that many students' basic needs are not met. This includes not just food and shelter but also access to a private bed, shower, and clean clothes. How do we, as educators who are with our students eight hours a day, give our students space for voice and agency within these circumstances? When a student is falling asleep in class for the fifth day in a row, do we nudge them and say, "Sleeping is for home, not for school" and simply leave it at that? When a student is sneaking a snack out of their pocket do you simply give them an unforgiving *put it away* look or do you check in with them to investigate if they had breakfast this morning? As I outline previously, students' ability to cultivate Self-Awareness and Self-Regulation is compromised when they are stuck in the panic of meeting their basic needs. As adults, we are the same way; we just have more resources to counter the anxiety of our basic needs not being met. If we had a restless night's sleep, we just swing by the faculty lounge for a cup of coffee. Some of our students may live in poverty where being hungry, tired, and having no option but unwashed clothes is a daily reality. Some students' resources are limited and so school becomes the place that can, and in my opinion is morally obligated to, help fill the gaps with a culturally responsive, equitable, and anti-racist approach that centers around the student and their needs.

If we unpack the idea of student well-being a bit further, we see that there are three essential questions to ask ourselves daily: Are our students' basic needs met? Does our classroom climate promote positive youth identity? And, are we taking responsibility for modeling healthy lifestyle choices for the students we spend hours with each day?

This topic can be triggering and I have occasionally heard educators say, "Geez, really!? I have to worry about teaching these kids academics *and* worry if they are hungry *and* worry if I drink too many Diet Cokes in front of them each day? Isn't this stuff the parents' job?" *Yes.* It is *also* the parents' and caregivers' job. But, if we believe we teach life-long learning skills, then it is our job, too.

A student who has a balance of protein and carbohydrates in the morning will perform differently than a student who has nutritionally void foods in the morning to fuel their day. Yet, how can we expect students to understand that sugar, caffeine, and nutritionally void foods negatively impact their learning? The best way to communicate healthy lifestyle choices—what to eat, what to drink, methods of exercise, ways to deal with stress, socially appropriate hygiene, screen time limits—is through what we, as educators, model each day.

Asking educators to model healthy choices can often be a delicate topic as they may be struggling with defining health and wellness for themselves. That being said, it is time for schools to draw a line in the sand: x is a healthy practice to model in front of students, y is not. (This principle should similarly apply to what is featured in the school store, sold for fundraisers, etc.) If we agree that educators are powerful role models, then we must also agree that adults should model healthy practices in front of students.

3

Pre-Teaching for Success

Starting with the Schedule

This schedule is meant to be adapted for early childhood classrooms. Educators may see students for a half or full day and should modify the schedule to meet their needs, being mindful to include ample **Come Together Time** to build classroom community.

8:30 am: Warm greeting upon arrival—Thumb Check student excitedly approaches his teacher with news to share.

Educator: *Thank you for letting me know, Hunter. When I announce Come Together Time, grab the Talking Stick and find a seat on the rug with criss-cross applesauce legs and hands in your lap.*

8:40 am: Children have table time with peer-to-peer chitchat. Whole-class Thumb Check or visit to POP Chart, three students at a time.

Thumb Check can be done at arrival or during table time. Choose what works for your classroom and then be consistent. As children arrive they are excited to be at school, hanging up coats, taking papers out of their bags, etc. Arrival may also include bathroom time. It is necessary that this transition from home to school is as structured and consistent as possible. (Don't forget to have a designated place for students to put papers from their backpacks and to have the table time activities ready to go. This will help minimize confusion or loss of instructional time.)

8:45 am: Table time (students continue to check in at POP Chart during this time).

Choices should include developmentally appropriate fine-motor activities (e.g., drawing, coloring, puzzles, blocks, Legos, beads, etc.). All children may be doing the same activity or different activities.

8:55 am: Provide a 2-minute warning. *Students, in 2 minutes, we will finish up what we are doing and meet on the rug. I am setting the timer now. We will be cleaning up in 2 minutes. I will let you know when 2 minutes are up and you need to stop what you are doing and put things away.*

8:57 am: *OK, my friends, time to put your things away. Please join me on the rug for Come Together Time when you are finished.* (The educator can be on the rug, and the aide can help those children who need assistance putting materials away.)

8:59 am: As the children come over to the rug area, teacher(s) and students sing the Hello Song together until everyone is settled. Teacher starts singing; children join in (movement can be added to keep all students engaged). Adults in the classroom (teachers, aides, etc.) should join the activity.

9:00 am: Come Together Time—Part 1 (Teaching SEL)

Come Together Time (CTT) is a daily whole-group activity that usually takes place on a rug or carpeted area. This time together is intended to be a positive, community-building experience. CTT is the foundation of our SEL early childhood curriculum. CTT lessons included during the first few months of school are intended to increase a child's ability to manage his or her own behavior, make smart choices, and use words to express the child's wants and needs in an appropriate manner.

Once all children are seated in appropriate places with the assistance of a teacher, then teachers will need a signal to get children quiet (Call and Response—"Okie"/"Dokie"—works really well here). Repeat as needed until children are settled on the rug in appropriate places. On average, CTT totals about 20–25 minutes per day, but it may be chunked to accommodate shorter attention spans. Typically early childhood teachers will have their students meet on the rug two or three times each day. Preschoolers are generally not able to sit for more than 10 or 15 minutes, which equals three 15-minute blocks (or two 20-minute blocks) of CTT each day. CTT is a flexible community-building session, and time allotted can depend on your students' age level.

This first session of CTT is dedicated to learning the yoga, movement, and relaxation activities posted in the POP Chart or Cool Down Corner. This session of CTT also includes a daily review of classroom rules, SEL concepts, social skills, etc. These SEL themes can be discussed during CTT and then practiced during work times and play throughout the day. An activity choice may be breath work like Lion's Breath or Listening Breath. Other options might be Mountain Pose, which requires focus and balance, or Star Pose, which allows for a lengthening stretch of the muscles.

A series of shared Agreements or classroom rules with accompanying motions will help keep behavior management to a minimum and learning to a maximum. For example: Teacher puts imaginary binoculars to her eyes and says *Eyes on the Action*. Students repeat and mimic the binoculars. Teacher says, *Listening Ears*, and cups her hands around both ears. Students echo her words and cup their own ears. Teacher says, *Belly Buttons to the Speaker*, and points her belly button and shoulders to her audience. Students say, *Belly buttons to the Speaker*, while they turn their whole bodies to face the teacher. Teacher says, *Criss-cross applesauce and hands in our laps*, while modeling this behavior in her own space. Students repeat and mimic her actions. Teacher says, *And now, we're ready to learn!* In less than 1 minute, the teacher and students together have recited the rules and set the tone for productive learning time.

9:20–10:15 am: Play

Your district or state may have specific requirements regarding minutes for play (indoor/outdoor, free play, structured play, centers, stations, etc.). If students are "playing" much of the day, this is your best opportunity to reinforce SEL skills. Play is also an excellent time to teach language, cognitive, and fine motor skills. Play is an ideal time for authentic learning/practicing of SEL skills and an excellent opportunity for observations and assessments.

10:15 am: Provide a 2-minute warning

10:17 am: Clean Up Song

10:25 am: Snack

Snacks can be provided during play in small groups or as a whole-group activity. Whole-group snack time is much preferred, as it is a wonderful way to practice language, cognitive, and social skills. A screen-free communal snack can encourage the manners around eating together and taking turns. This often does not happen in the children's homes. Counting, sharing, cooperation, asking, and answering questions all occur naturally during communal snack time. The community-building that snack time provides is invaluable and teachers should refrain from offering snacks as an optional center during free play (even though it may be easier).

10:35 am: Come Together Time—Part 2 (Song)

This second session of CTT is dedicated to connecting students through song. Tunes like "The More We Get Together," "Head Shoulders Knees and Toes," and "If You Are Happy and You Know It" (see Appendix) are excellent resources here. Given that it is later in your school day, students may fidget and lose interest in the lesson, so Echo and Mirror exercises will help keep the students' attention.

Once the second round of CTT has concluded, outdoor independent and small-group play time is ideal for observing students' SEL progress. Early childhood learners need time to practice the social skills they learn during stories and explicit lessons.

10:45 am: Outdoor or Indoor Time—Large Motor Movement

11:00 am: Home/Transition

Stating Expectations

Children need to know what the expectations are for learning. Transitioning from one activity to the next is often difficult for young children and requires clear pre-teaching and re-teaching. Consistent, structured practice is necessary to create a positive classroom climate for SEL to take place.

Explicitly teach the following concepts prior to the inclusion of movement during CTT. Empower your students with the Self-Awareness and Self-Regulation skills to manage their bodies and be successful.

Transitions

1. **Sitting on the Rug**
   Instruction happens from front of room, students' eyes and belly buttons track the speaker.
2. **Standing on the Rug**
   Children have more difficulty with Self-Regulation when they stand. Adding movement and music makes this even more difficult, especially on a small rug space. Giving children a large enough space in which to move is critical. Children need assistance with personal space.
3. **Scatter**
   Children need a Safe Space in the classroom for standing activities. Often, due to size, the rug is not the ideal place for movement. If children are too close to maintain personal space, teacher may cue, *Scatter* or *Find your Personal Space Spots*. At this point, students will locate a spot in the room where they can find their Safe Space Bubbles. Help students be successful by pre-teaching appropriate areas for Scatter. Often those children that need to be closest to the teacher take off to the furthest corners in the room!
4. **Lining Up**
   Line-up procedures (going to the bathroom, going outside, etc.) should be rehearsed and re-taught multiple times at the start of the school year to ease transition times.

Cues and Attention Getters

Those first days in your classroom lay down the foundation for learning. Children need structure with consistent expectations and consequences for appropriate and inappropriate behavior. Cues with short and simple wording help children respond quickly in an appropriate manner. At times, children may need to respond with voice and movement, voice alone, or just movement. Techniques that work well are Echo and Mirror and Call and Response. Understanding and following classroom rules are of major importance in an early childhood classroom. Children are encouraged and reminded of the rules on a daily basis and as needed. (Instead of, *I'm waiting for it to get quiet.* Try, *Zip Your Lips* or *Quiet Mouths and Bodies*. Children will Echo and Mirror these directions.) Eventually children will be able to follow the rules with minimal teacher assistance and stay actively involved in instruction.

A sample script to use the Echo and Mirror technique to teach the classroom rules during Come Together Time is presented here:

Friends, before we sing our Hello Song today, let's practice our classroom rules. Following these rules will help us get ready to learn. Remember, when we are on the rug together, we need to sit down on our bottoms and keep our hands and feet to ourselves. Now when I say criss-cross applesauce, you will echo me and say, criss-cross applesauce and you'll check to make sure your legs are crossed. Let's try it. Let's all say, criss-cross applesauce. [Educator repeats as needed.] *Great! Now it will be my turn first* [teacher points to self]*, so just listen. criss-cross applesauce! Now it is your turn.* [Educator gestures to children; the children repeat, criss-cross applesauce.] *Nicely done boys and girls!*

Now, let's practice Hands in your Laps. Let's say and do that together, Hands in our Laps. [Educator repeats as needed.] *Now, our next rule is Eyes on the Action.* [Teacher demonstrates circle eyes with fingers to form imaginary binoculars.] *That means look at me, because I'm talking right now. Let's say and do that together, Eyes on the Action.* [Educator repeats as needed.] *Nice work! Let's try that again. This time, it will be my turn first.* [Educator points to self.] *Eyes on the Action. Now it is your turn.* [Educator points to students.] *Eyes on the Action!*

OK, now girls and boys, we need to be good listeners. We need to have Listening Ears. [Educator cups hands behind ears.] *Let's all say and do that together, Listening Ears. Good. Let's try that again. This time, it will be my turn first.* [Educator points to self.] *Listening Ears.* [Educator points to children, they say Listening Ears.]

Our final rule is we need to be quiet when someone else is talking. Right now, I'm talking. Sometimes it will be your teacher's or your friend's turn to talk. Being quiet when someone is talking will help us get ready to learn. So, boys and girls, when someone is talking you need to Zip Your Lips. [Educator demonstrates pointer *finger and thumb drawing lips closed in zipper motion.] Let's all say and do that together, Zip Your Lips. Good job. Let's try that again. This time it will be my turn first.* [Educator points to self.] *Zip Your Lips.* [Uses zipping motion.] *Your turn!* [Educator points to children.] *Zip Your Lips.* [Children Echo and Mirror]. *Now we know our classroom rules! Nicely done!*

> **Educator Tip:** "My turn first" should always be paired with the teacher pointing to themselves, and "Your turn" should always be paired with pointing to children. This will become automatic with practice.

Call and Response

First-grade students may be ready for more than the Echo and Mirror technique. A more advanced group can use Call and Response, wherein the students respond in chorus with a memorized retort to the teacher's word or words. For example, the teacher says, "Okie," and the class responds, "Dokie!" The educator may say, "Hocus Pocus," and the class answers, "Time to focus!" I've also heard teachers use many variations of "Classsssss," and the students respond, "Yesssssss" (from Chris Biffle's *Whole Brain Teaching*). Variations include, with drawn out syllables, "Amigos: Maestra" and "Classity-class: Yessity-yes."

Call and Response is best used to get the children's attention and participation so children will be ready to learn.

Here is a sample script to teach Call and Response:

I'm going to teach you a signal. This is one of my favorites and it's fun to do. So, when I want you to be really good listeners, I'm going to say, "Okie" and show you this signal. [Educator joins thumb and index finger in a circle with remaining fingers pointing up.] *Then you are going to say, "Dokie" and show me the same signal.* [Educator again makes the OK gesture. Repeat a few times to get everyone's attention. Children may say both parts for this practice.]

Now we are going to take turns. I'll go first and then it will be your turn. My turn first [pointing to self], *Okie. Your turn* [pointing to children], *Dokie.* [Educator repeats as necessary.]

> **Educator Tip:** Support staff and paraprofessionals should model participation alongside the teacher. It is important for adults to respond with the children.

Foundational SEL: Teaching Body Awareness

Taking the time to pre-teach and re-teach body awareness is essential for the success of your classroom's approach to SEL. Body awareness is the foundation of Self-Awareness, which is the cornerstone of all SE competencies.

Quiet Feet, Quiet Hands

Quiet Feet, Quiet Hands is a Call and Response that can be used throughout the day. Teacher says, "Quiet Feet." Students respond, "Quiet Hands" and stand in Mountain Pose with hands and feet still.

A sample SEL script to teach Quiet Feet, Quiet Hands follows:

Boys and girls, today we are going to practice Quiet Feet and Quiet Hands. This means that you should sit or stand with your feet still and your arms still. This will help you get ready to learn.

So, my friends, let's practice. When you are sitting on the rug, you are sitting with quiet feet and quiet hands. You are sitting with your hands in your laps. When you stand up, I'm going to say, Quiet Feet, and make my feet very still. You are going to answer, Quiet Hands. When you answer, we are all going to make sure our feet and arms are still. Let's try this. 1, 2, 3: Everybody stand up. Remember, I'm going to say, Quiet Feet, and you are going to answer, Quiet Hands. I'll start. Quiet Feet. [Educator models. Children mirror. Children respond, "Quiet Hands". Repeat a few times. As students master Quiet Feet, Quiet Hands, they will be ready for Mountain Pose.] *This time, when I say Quiet Feet, I would like you to say Quiet Hands and freeze in Mountain Pose, standing up straight and tall with quiet feet and hands. Our feet are firmly on the ground. We are still and strong and silent like mountains.* [Educator practices cue with students.] *Nice work, boys and girls!*

Active Feet

Active Feet includes walking feet, marching feet, dancing feet, tiptoe feet, yoga feet, and so on. This is an echo-mirror that can be used throughout the day. For example, children may be transitioning from rug to tables. Educator says, "Tiptoe feet." Children respond, "Tiptoe feet," and tiptoe to tables.

A sample SEL script to teach Active Feet follows:

Friends, for the song we are going to do today, you will need active feet. Active Feet means your feet are moving. Today we are going to be dancing. Some of you will have dancing feet but not everyone likes to dance, so I want everyone to have Active Feet. Let me show you some ways your feet can be active. [Educator demonstrates marching feet and side-to-side feet.] *Some of you will also have Active Hands. It may be hard not to move your hands when you hear this song.*

Everyone, let's practice Active Feet. When I say, "Active Feet," you will Echo and Mirror. You will answer, "Active Feet," and you will start moving. Remember, everybody needs to move his or her feet.

Now I am going to need a helper. [Educator and helper practice appropriate behavior. Helper then shows class inappropriate behavior, in this case, no movement and then repeats the appropriate behavior. This can be repeated with the example of wild movement. Children often have difficulty controlling their bodies once they get moving.]

> **Educator Tip**: If the Safe Space Bubble has not been practiced, teachers will need to assist children to make sure they have personal space.
> Active Feet can also be used for transitions. Educators can pre-teach walking feet, marching feet, jumping feet, hopping feet, tiptoe feet, and heel walk for moving from place to place in the classroom. Educators can also take this opportunity to talk about running feet and when and where it is appropriate to have running feet.

Eyes on the Speaker

Belly Buttons and Eyes on the Speaker is a Call and Response cue to get children to turn their entire bodies to face the teacher. Teacher says, "Belly buttons." Children respond, "And eyes." This means the students' eyes and belly buttons are facing the teacher. The teacher may follow up by revisiting the classroom rules, if needed. Visiting classrooms, I have often observed children facing away from teachers with just their heads turned. When we teach, we need children to know we need whole-body attention.

A sample SEL script to teach Ready to Learn posture follows:

SEL Story—Friends, the story I want to tell you today is about how you can be ready to learn. We've already talked about our classroom rules. This is another important rule we need to practice whenever an adult is speaking.

When I'm talking, I need your Eyes on the Action, but I also need whole-body attention. This means I need your Belly Buttons and Eyes facing me. Let me show you. [Educator chooses a helper, either a teaching assistant or capable child.] *OK [Helper], I want you to be the teacher and I will be the student. Now I am going to look at you, Eyes on the Action and show you whole-body attention. My eyes and my belly button are facing you. How do I look everyone? Am I ready to learn?* [Students respond.]

OK, [Helper], now this time you are the teacher and I am going to look at you but my body is going to be facing toward the windows. Hmm, does this look like I'm ready to learn? No, this makes my neck hurt and I'm not comfortable. I can't really think, so I'm not really ready to learn.

What do I need to do? Belly Buttons and Eyes. Yes, turn my body and face the teacher. Thank you, [Helper].

Let's practice this together. So, when we are working together, I will say I need whole-body attention, Belly Buttons. You will answer, And Eyes. [Educator and students practice.]

> **Educator Tip:** This strategy can be used throughout the day to gain whole-body attention.

Circle Arms and Turn

If children do not have room to circle arms and turn then they do not have a Safe Space Bubble. This is a Call and Response cue and it can be used throughout the day. Teacher says, "Safe Space," and models, holding her hands together and elbows at shoulder level, turning at the waist. Children respond, "Bubble," and mirror the circling of their arms and twisting.

When children are seated too close to one another on the rug, the teacher cues, "Scoot back," with a "thumbs-up". This works really well if children are sitting in a circle. I have often observed children packed on the rug and expected to participate in movement. If this is the case, children will need to sit in another arrangement. If more space is needed, another option is a row of easily movable chairs behind the seated students and/or students sitting in rows on the rug. Take a good look at your rug area and make sure there is enough space for your students to engage in activities and have a Safe Space Bubble.

A sample SEL script to teach Safe Space Bubble follows:

Today we have a story to help us practice Safe Space when we are on the rug. What does Safe Space mean? Well, Mrs. X [Aide] and I are going to show you. When we sit down on the rug together in criss-cross applesauce we need to have our own Safe Space. Look, we're not touching each other, even if we make a circle with our arms and turn. We do not bump into each other. We are making a bubble. This will help us be good listeners and be ready to learn.

Now Mrs. X, I want to show the boys and girls what will happen if we are sitting too close to each other. Let's move close together. OK, now we will make our bubbles. Uh-oh. Trouble. [Educator puts hands up near face and makes a worried face.] *We bumped into each other, didn't we? How can we be good listeners if we are bumping into each other? I want my own Safe Space. How about you Mrs. X? Don't you want your own personal space?*

Now Mrs. X, when we are sitting too close all we need to do to solve this problem is Scoot back, [making the hitchhiker thumb gesture]. *Let's do that.* [Teachers look at each other, say, "Scoot back," show thumb, and scoot back.] *Now, let's check to make sure we have our own Safe Space.* [Educators look at each other, say, "Safe Space: Bubble," circle their arms and twist.] *What do you think Mrs. X, are we ready to learn?* [To help students be successful, teachers should assist the children with personal space.]

Now friends, it's your turn. Let's check to see if you are each in your own Safe Space. I will say, Safe Space. You will answer, Bubble, and circle your arms and turn. Ready? Safe Space. [Children respond, "Bubble." Children circle their arms and turn to both sides.] *Good! Let's do that again.* [Repeat.]

OK, it is time to test out our Safe Space Bubbles! I think we're ready to try a little breath work. This activity is called Sunrise Breath. [You may want to show a picture of the sun rising as an additional visual cue.] *The sun comes up in the morning. The sun is rising up into the sky. My turn first: I'm going to breathe in as my arms rise up, and my fingers touch each other to form the sun. As I breathe out, my arms travel back down to my sides. Watch me again.* [Repeat.] *Now, my friends, it is your turn. 1, 2, 3, breathe in, arms up, make your sun, breathe out arms down.* [Repeat two more times.] *Now, we come back to Mountain Pose with Quiet feet and Quiet hands.*

> **Educator Tip:** When seated or standing on the rug, there should be visual cues to assist with the Safe Space concept, for instance, carpet squares, sectioned boxes, etc. If possible, children should be seatedor standing in a circle. This formation promotes attention and participation.

Safe Touch[1]

Safe touch is an important concept for early childhood learners to understand. Safe touch empowers students to create boundaries with adults and peers around how, when, and where they should be touched. By helping students cultivate body awareness they can learn to touch—and be touched—in a safe way. The following is a scripted lesson to help educators give students the words to create boundaries with adults or children when touch does not feel safe.

The rules of safe touch apply at school and at home. Just because someone is related to you, a close friend, or an adult you trust, does not mean that they can touch you in a way that makes your body feel uncomfortable or is unsafe.

For me, safe touch is . . .

Head to Shoulders. [Educator motions toward head, moves down to shoulders.]

Shoulders to Hands. [Educator motions toward shoulders, moves down to hands.]

Knees to Feet. [Educator motions toward knees, moves down to feet.] Students and teacher repeat sequence three times.

If you have not already, this is a great opportunity to discuss consent with your students. (i.e. "Do I have permission to touch your shoulder?" "Yes, you may touch my shoulder. But, please do not . . .") Our sense of what our boundaries are and what we consider safe touch is often formed in childhood. People who have experienced trauma or abuse often have a difficult time establishing boundaries or having conversations about consent. Victims of trauma or abuse can grow into adulthood having never learned what boundaries are or what they look like for themselves or someone else.

It is very important that you learn to how to say "No" and "Stop" to adults and children when you feel unsafe or someone is touching your body in a way that does not feel right. Do not assume that adults or other students in your life have boundaries and practice safe touch simply because they are older than you or because they seem OK.

If it is difficult for you to say "NO" to someone, say "Stop. Now!" and leave immediately. Do not worry if they feel bad. No one's feelings are more important than your own. Leave immediately and tell a caring adult whom you trust what happened.

Now, let's think of how we can use safe touch when we are playing in centers. Everyone, if you want to talk to a friend, you can do two things. You can use your words, or you can try Gentle Tap. Let me show you what I mean. I am going to need a helper. OK, Helper, let's pretend that you are playing with blocks on the rug. [Use actual blocks.] *Now, I want to play with you. I walk up to you, but you are so busy playing you don't see me. What can I do?*

First, I'm going to try to use my words. Can I play with you? [Helper doesn't respond.] *Hmm, that didn't work. I know! Maybe if I say my friend's name first, then she will know that I'm talking to her. I'm going to try that. Helper, can I play with you?* [Helper responds by looking up at the teacher and saying, "Sure."]

So, boys and girls, saying her name first helped, didn't it? I don't think Helper knew I was talking to her.

Now let's try this again. This time I'm going to show you Gentle Tap.

Helper, can I play with you? [Helper doesn't respond.] *I can try using my words again.* [Helper still doesn't respond.] *That still didn't work. Now I will try Gentle Tap. If I am going to tap my friend, I think the best place to give her a tap would be on her shoulder. That's a safe touch. I'm going to try this.* [Educator walks up to Helper and practices safe touch. Helper looks up and teacher asks, "Can I play with you?' Helper responds, "Sure."]

So, if you want to get a friend to listen to you, try to use your words or try Gentle Tap. Thank you for being such great listeners, everyone. Nice job!

> **Educator Tip**: This is a great time to use the Safe Space Bubble technique or to discuss personal space. Personal space can be practiced while children are seated on the rug or standing. The concept is the same. Seated personal space is taught first, followed by standing with quiet feet and hands, to standing with active feet and/or arms. Introducing and practicing the concept of safe touch or personal space reinforces SE competencies like Self-Awareness.

Note

1. Readers, if you have a difficult time setting personal or physical boundaries and/or you have been the victim of unsafe touch, you may find teaching this concept to be triggering or emotionally challenging. Please practice grace with yourself, take time to heal, and seek out an ally, if needed.

4

SEL-Informed Classroom

The components outlined here are invaluable in your adaptive SEL-Informed classroom (Figure 4.1). These tools should be pre-taught and re-taught to help guarantee student success. *Teacher cues for each activity are in italic type, for ease of implementation.*

- **Classroom Agreements and POP Chart** (Figure 4.2): Practices to ensure students have space to own their feelings, recognize and express their needs, and build a strong, interpersonal relationship with a caring adult
- **Sample Schedule** (Figure 4.3): To help teachers create a consistent safe classroom
- **Talking Stick**: An Indigenous practice to ensure equity of voice during whole-group discussions

Like adults, kids have legitimate concerns: hunger, fatigue, fear, a desire to do certain things, a desire for approval, a tendency to avoid things they are not good at, a desire not to be embarrassed or humiliated, and so forth.

Ross Greene (2014)

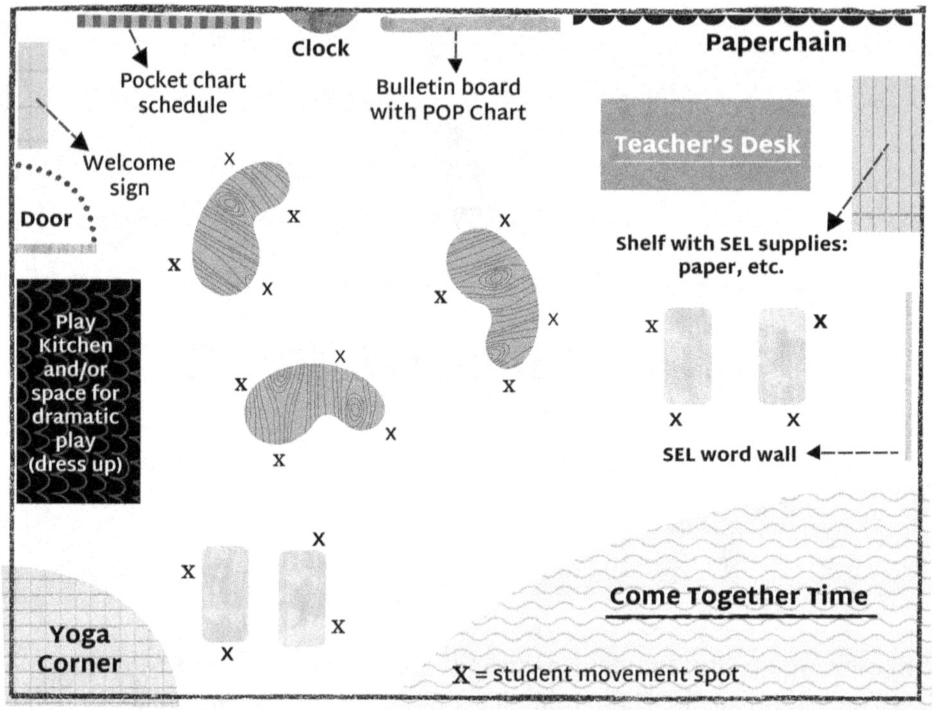

56 ◆ SEL-Informed Classroom

Figure 4.1 The SEL Classroom

Intentionality is key to an SEL-informed classroom. When done well, SEL implementation positively impacts a classroom's climate and culture. An observer can see it, hear it, and feel it as soon as they enter the room. The POP Chart gives students space to PAUSE (breathe and check-in), OWN IT (name their emotions/feelings), and PRACTICE (a solution) being present and aware in the moment.

Some key questions to consider:

- When will your students use or reference the POP Chart and how will it connect with your classroom procedures and routines? (At the start of the school day? After lunch or recess?)
- When you don't have your POP Chart handy, how can you use a quick Thumb Check with your students? (On the playground? In the bathroom line?)
- Where can you set up the POP Chart so that students can access it throughout the school day if they need additional support?

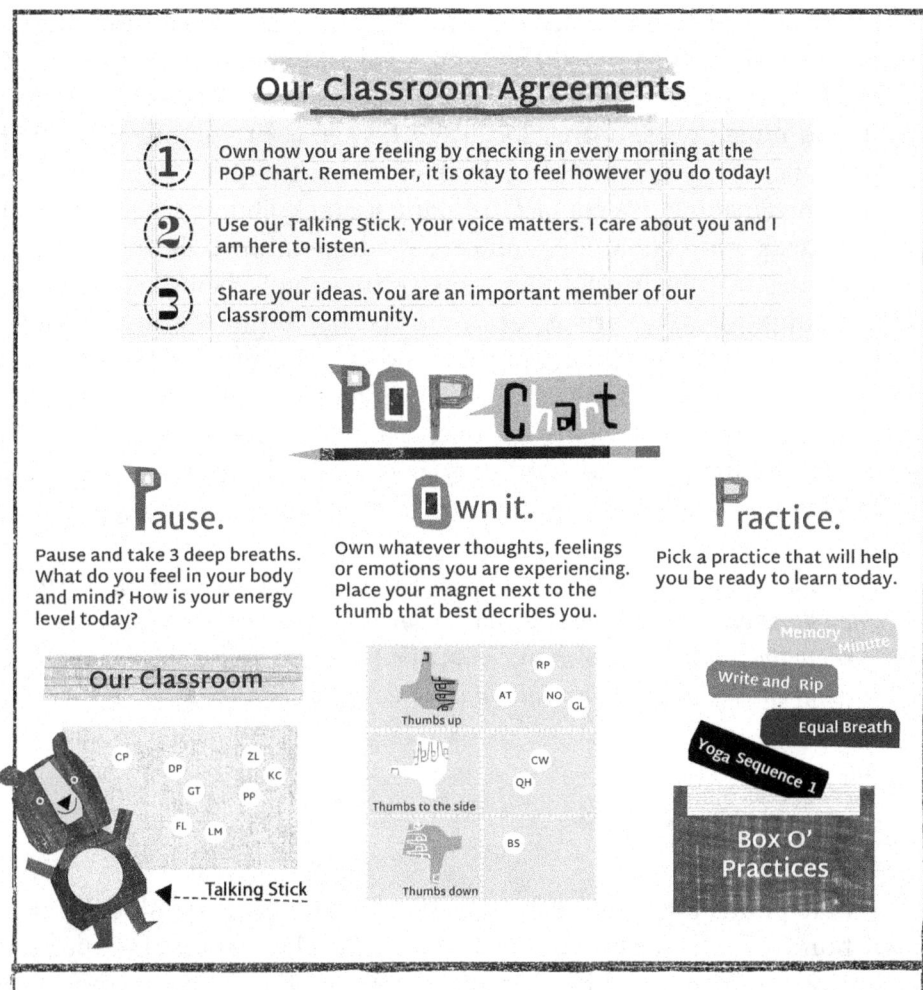

Figure 4.2 The SEL Wall

Thumb Check: All Hands On Deck

Thumb Checks are a quick and simple way to give students an opportunity to assess their own feelings and body sensations in the moment, and for the educator to get a measure of the students' mood and energy levels. I recommend that all school stakeholders check in with students as they enter the building at the start of each school day. For many classroom teachers, students may walk in the door and go right to the POP Chart. For others, they might greet their students with a Thumb Check at the door, and then cue students to go to the POP Chart after they put their backpacks away.

The wonderful thing about a Thumb Check is that it is a tool that an entire school staff can use quickly and easily to check in with students, whether they are in or out of the classroom. For instance, from 7:45 am to 7:55 am, administrators, deans, social workers, parent volunteers, custodians, and lunchroom staff could be in the hallways with students, greeting them warmly, making eye contact, utilizing a quick Thumb Check. This all-hands-on-deck approach utilizes all caring adults in the building and communicates to students that nothing—answering emails, being on the phone, entering grades, texting, or squeezing in that last bit of lesson planning—trumps the importance of being present and emotionally available for their student community. It is a shared expectation for each and every adult in the building, encouraging students to build lasting interpersonal relationships with caring adults who are not necessarily their classroom teacher. This also gives school stakeholders a chance to work together to support their students.

Hi, Ms. Jimenez. I connected with Takia as she entered school this morning. She mentioned she is having a Thumbs-Down day and that there has been some trouble at home. I know that you coach her in soccer and that you two have a great relationship. Do you mind checking in with her later during your practice?

Building Relational Trust

At multiple points throughout the day, an educator may ask students for a quick Thumb Check. The purpose of a Thumb Check is to build interpersonal relationships between students and adults through the consistent practice of processing and giving voice to feelings and emotions. For educators, it is also a practical way to gauge students' mood and energy levels for optimal learning. The educator simply signals the students to hold their thumbs against their chests, which is quick and easy if the class is transitioning between activities, if there is a school assembly, or if a student is interacting with a teacher one-on-one.

Thumbs-Up: I'm experiencing pleasant feelings: calm, relaxed, happy
Thumbs to the Side: Meh. I'm bored, restless, distracted
Thumbs-Down: I'm experiencing unpleasant feelings: sad, mad, stressed, hungry

Giving your students multiple methods to check in with you or a caring adult demonstrates that you are invested in building relational trust with your students.

Encourage all school stakeholders, parents, administrators, and staff to check in with students at any point during the day with a quick Thumb Check. Create time and space for Thumbs-Down students to act with agency and find a solution, whether it is an activity from the POP Chart or a simple breathing activity to help them regulate and be present.

Some early childhood students may consistently display Thumbs-Down just for the attention it garners. Do not dismiss a Thumbs-Down signal, however; this is a great conversation starter with a young learner who may be in need but does not yet have the words to articulate their thoughts, feelings, or emotions.

POP Chart: Intrapersonal + Interpersonal

As students enter your classroom, give them 3 minutes of music to get their materials organized and visit the **POP Chart**.

Provide each student with a magnet decorated with their picture, initials or first name on the front. As part of the morning routine, after hanging coats and book bags, each student moves their magnet to the appropriate place on the chart: Thumbs-Up, Thumbs to the Side, or Thumbs-Down. As the music plays, students PAUSE to check in with how they are feeling. Then, they OWN IT by moving their name magnets to indicate their emotions or feelings. Lastly, they choose an activity to PRACTICE that will help them be present for the day ahead. When the music is over, the students are at their tables engaged in independent work and ready to learn.

> **PAUSE**: Pause and take 3 deep breaths. What do you feel in your body and mind? How is your energy level today?
> **OWN IT**: Own whatever thoughts, feelings or emotions you are experiencing. Place your magnet next to the thumb that best describes you.
> **PRACTICE**: Pick a practice that will help you be ready to learn today.

For those individual students who have moved their magnets to indicate they are having a difficult day, find a time during instruction to connect with that student and offer a SEL or mindfulness practice that would meet their needs. Sometimes, they just might need to connect with an adult. Ask permission to extend a hug or find a little time to chitchat.

As children arrive and take care of their morning routines, they may choose to check in at the POP Chart first thing or they may want to go to table time first. The rule might be "POP-3," or, only three children at the chart at one time. An aide or paraprofessional may be stationed nearby to assist with the POP Chart arrival routine for the first few weeks.

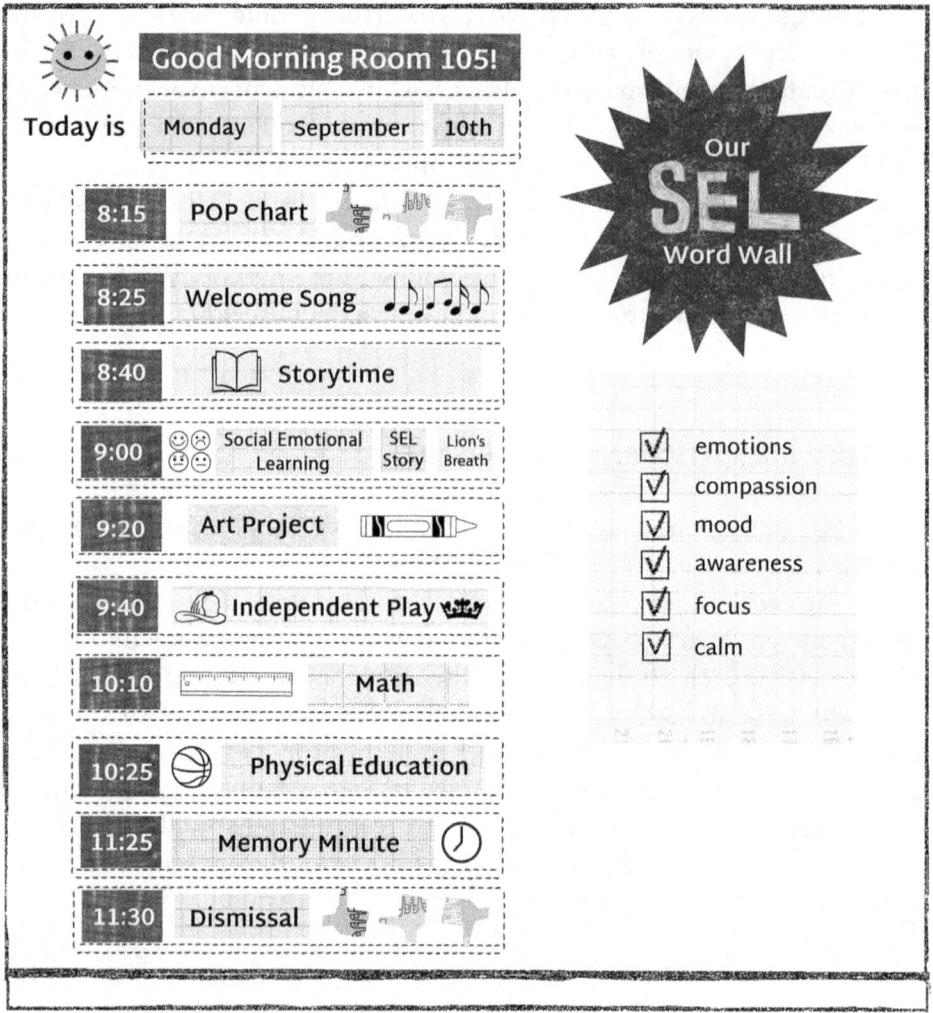

Figure 4.3 Daily SEL Schedule

It is recommended that the educator set clear expectations with students to help ensure that the POP Chart check-in routine is a smooth, fluid, and safe process. Whole-class implementation (Tier 1) is preferred, with extended time in the POP Chart for students with exceptionalities or who need assistance modifying their behavior throughout the day. These additional minutes can be added to the POP Chart check-in to give students extra processing time.

Protocols and Procedures

Once the POP Chart has been set up, it is important to take the time to walk students through their daily routine prior to implementation, as many of the check-ins will take place during non-instructional time before academics begin. Model the strategies for the students, demonstrating how to perform a Thumb Check or use an activity in the POP Chart. As Harry Wong points out in his *Facilitator's Handbook* (2009), consistently practiced classroom routines at the start of the school year can be the key to student success. Have activities posted clearly as part of your daily schedule. As one of the goals of the POP Check is to build the interpersonal relationship between the student and teacher, reinforce an SEL-informed classroom environment by being transparent and consistent.

Any time a new activity is learned, a visual for that activity should be added to the POP Chart. That way, you and the students can have access to the activity when needed. To build student ownership of the POP Chart, encourage them to suggest activities that they have tried outside of your class. Visuals are very important, as they make the activities accessible to all learners.

Post procedures for taking a break next to the POP Chart. Clearly establish your expectations for POP Chart behavior (i.e., Do students raise their hand to ask if they can get out of their seats and walk over to the POP Chart? What is the procedure if more than one student wants to visit the POP Chart at a time? Are there any times when the POP Chart is closed to visitors?).

Step 1: Sit or stand facing the POP Chart and set the timer for 3 minutes.
Step 2: Choose one activity to practice.
Step 3: When the timer goes off, stop the activity and return to your seat.

Create a Comfortable Space

Your POP Chart can be a place for a student to be alone with their thoughts, or to reset when they are having a difficult time making positive choices. Comfortable bean bags, cushions, and pillows all make for a restful, relaxing place to reset. Display visuals of breathing exercises, yoga poses, and movement activities from which the students can choose to calm down and focus. A basket of picture books should be accessible, too.

Use Cases

> The indispensable foundation for success in every endeavour is the right state of mind. The same is true for learning. To help people learn better, the first task is to support them in acquiring the optimal state of mind; namely, Relaxed Alertness.
>
> Rick Reis, Stanford

The educator scripts that follow are in *italic type* to assist you in creating a climate and culture that is optimal for learning. These scripts help illustrate *use cases* for both the Thumb Check and POP Chart. Examples of what the practices can sound like and how to nurture the right state of mind or what Caine etal. (2016) call *relaxed alertness*, where the learner is both relaxed and emotionally available for the learning process. By consistently using Thumb Checks and the POP Chart with your students, you can bring your classroom together daily in a centered, present, and compassionate climate.

Frenetic Energy

It is the week before Winter Break and the teacher notices her class is unusually frenetic. Instead of using shaming language such as "I cannot believe what a crazy class we are today!" the teacher recruits the students' help in finding a solution to set her class up for a successful group work activity.

OK, Room [x], I notice we have a lot of extra energy this morning. Let's use a relaxation activity to help us be present and focused. [Student name] what activity from our **POP Chart** *do you think could help us calm down? [Student responds. Teacher facilitates activity.] Great job, scholars! Before we transition to the rug, I would like to get a quick* **Thumb Check**. *[Students hold thumbs up to chest, teacher takes a moment to process where the energy of the class is and whether they need another activity or are ready to continue with their assignment.] Thank you, class. It looks like we are relaxed and ready to learn. Nice job!*

Worried Students

The class is going back to remote learning for a month and the teacher knows her students would benefit from a bit of yoga or physical movement to help process feelings of stress and anxiety.

The new schedule starts on Monday and I know that a few of us are anxious. I noticed that most students entered the room this morning and placed their magnet next to 'Meh' on the **POP Chart**. *Thank you for sharing your feelings. I care about you and want to do all I can to help our class with our worries. [Student x], please lead our class through your favorite POP Chart activity, to help us be calm and relaxed today.*

Lethargic Learners

Room [x], I notice our energy is low, and we still have our alphabet folders to work on today. Let's use an SEL activity to energize our bodies and get ready to learn. [Student name], can you name a **POP Chart** *activity that will help energize our* *class and stimulate our brains?* [Student leads the class through the selected activity.] *Nicely done, Room [x]. Before we transition back to our alphabet folders, I would like to get a quick* **Thumb Check** *from our room.* [Students hold thumbs up to chest, teacher takes a moment to process where the energy of the class is and whether they need another activity or are ready to continue with their assignment.] *Thank you, class. Now, we are energized and ready to try our best!*

POP Chart and Student Agency

Post your POP Chart in a location where children will have the opportunity to move their magnets throughout the day. A child may start off the day with a Thumbs-Down but want to move to a different feelings report as the day progresses. The educator will need to check in with children throughout the day as they observe positive and negative behaviors. Verbal cues for appropriate and inappropriate behavior may be used, such as *Uh-oh, trouble*. This could be used as a signal to a student that it's time to check in at the POP Chart. Some educators already may have an area in their classrooms such as a Cool Down Corner to take a break, talk about feelings, and calm down. Given the space, time, and permission, children will begin to understand their feelings and act with voice and agency to construct solutions.

A daily interaction utilizing the POP Chart may look something like this:

During free play Marley gets upset, Benny won't let her play with him. Marley pushes him. Benny screams and tells the teacher, "Marley pushed me."

Teacher says "Uh-oh, trouble," assesses the situation, tries to get the whole story, and then says, "Benny, Marley and I are going to talk it out at the POP Chart. We'll be back to talk to you in a few minutes." Teacher walks Marley over to the POP Chart.

Teacher asks Marley "Can you tell me what happened?" Now Marley may answer, "I don't know," or she may be able to explain. Teacher reviews the episode and shows understanding of how Marley felt when she pushed Benny. Teacher says, "I want to talk you through this and help you make a smart choice the next time this happens. So, let's pause, stop for a moment, and take a breath. Now let's talk about what happened." Teacher accepts Marley's explanation and shows understanding of her feelings. Children need their feelings validated and then need to settle down with a POP Chart choice like breath work or a sequence of yoga poses.

Once the child has settled down and practiced an activity from the POP Chart, the teacher invites Benny over to join them at the POP Chart. Marley apologizes, "I am sorry I pushed you, Benny. Next time I will use my words."

Teacher will then help children find appropriate words. Teacher may suggest, "I will talk instead of hit," or "I will ask for help from a teacher." Children will be encouraged to expect appropriate behavior and to never accept inappropriate behavior as being "OK."

Benny may also need time to problem-solve with the teacher on how he can use his words to find his power. "What do I do if I want to play by myself?" Or, "What do I do if someone hurts me?"

POP Chart Check-Ins

You can cue a student at any point throughout the day to utilize a POP Chart activity, if they need to take a moment to relax and focus. Wherever they may be, honor where students are and move their energy toward calm and ready to learn.

Sun-Hi, I noticed your body is wiggly and that you are having a difficult time focusing during our Circle Time today. Please go to the POP Chart and choose an activity that will help you focus. Please set the timer for 2 minutes.

A process like this can empower a student with the choice and agency that comes with cultivating Self-Awareness and Self-Regulation skills, instead of simply disciplining them for being wiggly during Circle Time. It is important that the student owns the shift in their energy, not the educator who casually observes, "OK, fine. It looks like you are x, y or z." Even if it takes a bit more effort, try your best to give your students the space to understand their emotions and how to regulate them rather than jumping to conclusions about what *you think* they may be feeling or experiencing.

Crafting General Classroom Agreements

The following are sample Agreements to use as a platform to build consensus among your students around the use of the POP Chart and other classroom activities. The Agreements help students co-create their school experience with voice and agency. The Agreements should be signed by all class members, as well as all adults and teachers, and hung next to the POP Chart (see Figure 4.2).

Our Classroom Agreements

1. Own how you are feeling by checking in every morning at the POP Chart. Remember, it is okay to feel however you do today!
2. Use our Talking Stick. Your voice matters. I care about you and I am here to listen.
3. Share your ideas. You are an important member of our classroom community.

If you would also like to create Agreements for individual activities or to reinforce classroom norms, use the script here to help promote student voice and agency. (It can often be helpful to create the Agreements after the directions of the activity have been introduced but prior to when the activity itself begins.)

Before we begin [x activity], I need to find a student who is demonstrating our be the solution behavior by sitting up tall, with two feet flat on the floor, hands folded, and respecting their neighbor's personal space, who can restate our new activity in their own words. [Educator calls on student demonstrating the expectations. Student restates activity.]

Thank you, [Student name]. Room [x], do we see any potential problems with implementing this activity? [Educator calls on one or two students to discuss potential pitfalls.]

Thank you, [Student names]. So, now that we know where the problems may occur, how can we be the solution? What Agreements do we need to make for the activity to be physically and emotionally safe for all? What are the consequences if the Agreements are broken?

> **Educator Tip**: In an SEL-informed classroom, it is imperative that you consistently uphold the Agreements.

We have time for [x number of] students to share their thoughts. Before we share, let's remember to listen intently to others, accept others' opinions, and be careful not to interrupt our classmates. [Educator calls on students and writes the Agreements and consequences on the board. This is also the perfect time for the teacher to suggest modifications to the activity for students with limited physical mobility, students with self-esteem challenges, students who are deaf and hard of hearing, English language learners, and students with exceptionalities.]

Thank you, [Student names]. Now that we have our Agreements and consequences on the board, let's Check for Understanding.[1] *Please raise your right hand in the air. A "high-five" hand tells me you understand the activity, our Agreements, and the consequences if the Agreements are broken, and you are all set to begin. Two fingers in the air, or a peace sign, tells me that you have a question or comment that needs to be addressed before we begin. A fist in the air tells me that you are unsure and you are not ready to begin, which is OK. It is important that we have created a physically and emotionally safe classroom environment for our activity to take place.*

[Educator reads room and responds appropriately to student needs by answering questions, restating activity, building consensus, etc.]

Thank you, Room [x], for sharing your thoughts respectfully and thoughtfully. I witnessed students actively listening to their peers. Well done! Now, let's move on to our activity, [x]!

Talking Stick

Talking Stick is an Indigenous practice utilizing a passed object to facilitate equity of voice. The student who is holding the "stick" gets to speak while the other students are active and engaged listeners. Although this can be a simple practice, I recommend crafting Agreements to guarantee that this activity is equitable for all. These Agreements can extend to general sharing, circle time, or large group discussions.

It is recommended that you visually display your Talking Stick Agreements and place them next to the POP Chart in your classroom. While each grade level will have differences, the following are a few ideas to include in the Talking Stick Agreements:

- The student holding the Talking Stick is the only one to speak.
- The Talking Stick is passed silently from student to student (often in a circle). The Talking Stick is not to be thrown.
- Students must wait until each student has had a chance to share before they request to speak again. The teacher should let the students know that there may not be enough time for everyone to have another turn. Alternatively, students can choose to "pass" anytime.
- The speaker must use "I" language and talk only about their experiences.
- The teacher should conclude the Talking Stick circle with a Thumb Check before transitioning to the next activity.

> **Educator Tip**: Make the Talking Stick available to students when they first arrive to your class each day. Depending on what is happening outside of the schoolhouse or classroom doors, they may walk in with information to process. Giving them a positive outlet to share that information not only builds relational trust and Social Awareness, it also gives students the tools to be present.

Note

1 Adapted from Doug Lemov's *Check for Understanding*.

5

Framing SEL

Introducing SEL: Days 1–3

This chapter begins with three days of scripted lessons for introducing SEL to your students. Taking the time to pre-teach the concepts is essential for the success of any SEL approach. Diving immediately into the SEL, mindfulness, and yoga activities, without taking the time to lay the foundation, will potentially leave the students feeling confused and vulnerable. As with the other scripted lessons in this book, it is *not* recommended that you read the script aloud word-for-word, as that would not help develop your competency as a practitioner. Instead, the script is meant to be a reflective guide that provides a solid idea of how the content is framed, paced, and managed. Read the script a few times, take notes, and then make it your own.

Day 1: SEL and Classroom Practices

I am excited because this week begins Social Emotional Learning! I am looking for students respecting our classroom Agreements to make a prediction of what Social Emotional Learning, or SEL, is. [Educator calls on students demonstrating the Agreements. Students guess definition of SEL. Educator writes keywords on the board.]
   Let's break down the name Social Emotional Learning. Social is being with your classmates, friends, family, teachers, and adults at school and in your community!

So, to help us remember Social, let's stretch our arms out wide, like this. [Educator stretches arms out wide, students follow.]

Emotional refers to all the feelings and emotions we experience and our awareness of them (intrapersonal), and all the feelings and emotions we experience and our awareness of them when we engage with other kids or adults (interpersonal). Like how it is important to be kind to ourselves, so then we can learn to be kind to others. To help us remember Emotional, we will put two hands over our hearts. [Educator models, students follow.]

The last part of the name is Learning: Social Emotional Learning; learning about our behavior and interactions with others along with our feelings and emotions. But, since this is a school, the word Learning also has a special meaning. Here, Learning can also mean how our mood and energy or our interactions with others influence us as learners. For instance, is it harder for us to learn and concentrate if we have a fight at recess? Or, is it harder for us to learn and concentrate if we skipped breakfast? So, for the word Learning, let's put hands on the top of our heads. [Educator models, students follow.]

Let's practice the entire sequence two times together: Social [Educator and students stretch their arms out wide], *Emotional* [Educator and students put two hands over their hearts], *Learning* [Educator and students put hands on the top of their heads].

Nice job, Room [x]! I see everyone participating and trying their best! Let's practice our Social Emotional Learning sequence one more time: Social [Educator and students stretch their arms out wide], *Emotional* [Educator and students put two hands over their hearts], *Learning* [Educator and students put hands on the top of their heads]. *Great job, everyone!*

Social Emotional Learning is the process through which we develop Self-Awareness—being aware of how emotions and feelings affect our bodies and minds and influence how we make decisions. Social Emotional Learning helps us look at how the consequences of our actions affect our classmates, our school, and ourselves. By studying Social Emotional Learning, we can self-regulate—or make more positive, kind choices about our behavior—so that we can be kind toward others and ourselves.

Social Emotional Learning helps us understand our emotions so we can calm down, focus, and control our behavior so we are always ready to learn!

All the practices that we learn during our Social Emotional Learning time will be added to our POP Chart, so we can use them any time we need a break. Remember, the POP on our chart stands for "PAUSE—OWN IT—and PRACTICE." This is how we approach our feelings and emotions during our morning check-in routine each day. [Educator walks to center and points to pocket chart.] *Let's review our POP Chart!*

In the morning, we go to the POP Chart as part of our daily routine. First, you will PAUSE to notice what you are feeling. Then, you OWN what you are feeling, by placing your magnet next to the thumb that best depicts your emotion that day. Lastly, you will find a PRACTICE that best meets your needs in the moment so you can be ready to learn.

For instance, let's say you are checking in tomorrow morning, after you had a fight with your sister at breakfast. You PAUSE and notice that the emotion you are coming to school with is anger, because you are still upset about fighting with her. So, you OWN your emotions and place your magnet next to the Thumbs-Down picture, which communicates to your classmates and teachers that you are upset. [Educator demonstrates.]

Next, you will find the activities in the PRACTICE column that can help you calm down and be ready to learn. Any time you are stressed, it is important to take a moment to be kind and compassionate with yourself. When we take a moment to be kind to ourselves, it is easier to let go of anger or bad feelings.

It is important that you go to the POP Chart each morning. That way, you always have an opportunity to PAUSE and name the emotion you are feeling, instead of carrying it with you all day. By OWNING IT you are able to find the right SEL activity to PRACTICE, so that you can cool down, focus, and be ready to learn.

Let's review! Step 1 is PAUSE and notice what you are feeling in the body and in the mind. Step 2 is OWN IT, whatever you are feeling in the body and in the mind. Put your magnet by the Thumbs-Up, Thumbs to the Side, or Thumbs-Down picture that best describes where you are today. Step 3, PRACTICE the activity on the POP Chart that will help you focus and be ready to learn.

Sometimes, I will say that our class needs to practice a POP Chart activity together. At other times, I might ask that you go to the POP Chart on your own to practice an activity before you rejoin the group. For instance, I might say to one of you, "I notice you are having a difficult time honoring your neighbor's personal space. Please go to the POP Chart to choose an activity to help you make a more positive choice about your behavior." Then, you will choose an activity that will help you focus. When you feel you are ready, you will rejoin our class.

As I mentioned before, there are three different situations when we can visit the POP Chart to practice those activities.

The first is during our morning check-in routine, when we all PAUSE to notice what we are feeling, OWN what we are feeling by naming the feeling or emotion, and PRACTICE an activity that can help us relax and be ready to learn.

The second is any time our class needs to do an activity together to focus and calm down.

The third is any time you need to take a moment to control your behavior, you raise your hand and ask to go to the POP Chart.

Day 2: Reviewing SEL

Yesterday we learned about Social Emotional Learning or SEL. I am looking for students respecting our classroom rules to tell me, in their own words, what Social Emotional Learning is. [Educator calls on students demonstrating the expectations. Students restate definition of SEL. Educator writes keywords on the board.]

Very nice, Room [x]! Let's practice our Social Emotional Learning sequence together: Social [Educator and students stretch their arms out wide], *Emotional* [Educator and students put one hand over their hearts, then give themselves a hug], *Learning* [Educator and students put hands on the top of their heads]. *I am looking for a student who is demonstrating our be the solution behavior who can come to the front of the room and lead our class through our SEL sequence.* [Educator chooses student, student leads class through sequence.] *Great job, everyone! Let's try that one more time!* [Student leads class through sequence again.]

Nice work, Room [x]. I saw students respecting their neighbor's personal space. Let's remember that Social Emotional Learning is the process by which we develop Self-Awareness—how emotions and feelings affect our bodies and minds and influence how we make decisions. Social Emotional Learning helps us look at how the consequences of our actions affect our classmates, our school, and ourselves. By studying Social Emotional Learning, we can Self-Regulate—or make more positive, kind choices about our behavior—so that we can be compassionate toward ourselves and others. Social Emotional Learning helps us understand our emotions so we can calm down and focus.

Let's take a moment to review our Social Emotional Learning morning POP Chart check-in! Step 1 is to PAUSE and notice what you are feeling in your body and mind. Step 2 is to OWN it by placing your magnet by the Thumbs-Up/Thumbs to the Side/Thumbs-Down that best describes your emotion. Step 3, PRACTICE an activity on the POP Chart that will help you focus and get ready to learn.

Some of us like movement to help us get ready to learn, and some of us like breathing or relaxation activities to help us focus. Each of us is built differently and has different needs. The most important thing is to be aware of our needs so that we can make positive choices.

I am now looking for two students to tell me the three ways we practice SEL in Room [x]. [Educator calls on students. Students give examples of how the POP Chart can be utilized throughout the day.] *Well done, Room [x]!*

After we learn a new Social Emotional Learning activity, we will write it on a sentence strip and add it to our POP Chart so that we can practice it any time our class needs help dealing with a stressful situation or getting along with peers. The POP Chart is here to help us positively deal with our emotions so that we can always be ready, even in tough situations.

Let's review the activities in our POP Chart. [Educator walks over to center and names activities.] *Practicing these activities as part of our morning check-in routine helps us remember that we are in charge of our own behavior.*

Before we practice our SEL activity, I am looking for a student who can tell me what Social Emotional Learning is in their own words. [Educator chooses one student to restate definition.] *Now, may I have another volunteer to explain why we need Social Emotional Learning in school?* [Educator chooses another student to share their thoughts.] *Great work, scholars!*

Day 3: Reviewing the Why

These last few days we have learned about Social Emotional Learning or SEL. I am looking for a students to tell me, in their own words, what Social Emotional Learning is. [Educator calls on students demonstrating the expectations. Students restate definition of SEL. Educator writes keywords on the board.] *Well done, Room [x]!*

I am now looking for students who can tell me the three ways we practice SEL in Room [x]. [Educator calls on students. Students give examples of different ways to utilize the POP Chart throughout the day.]

Well done, Room [x]. Let's practice our Social Emotional Learning sequence together: Social [Educator and students stretch their arms out wide], *Emotional* [Educator and students put one hand over their hearts, then give themselves a hug], *Learning* [Educator and students put hands on the top of their heads]. *I am looking for a student who would like to come to the front of the room and lead our class through our SEL sequence.* [Educator chooses student, student leads class through sequence.] *Great job, everyone! Let's try that one more time!* [Student leads class through sequence again.]

Very nice, Room [x]! Let's remember that Social Emotional Learning is the process through which we develop Self-Awareness—how emotions and feelings affect our bodies and minds and influence how we make decisions. Social Emotional Learning helps us look at how the consequences of our actions impact our classmates, our school, and ourselves. By studying Social Emotional Learning, we can self-regulate— or make more positive, kind choices about our behavior—so that we can be compassionate toward others and ourselves. Social Emotional Learning helps us understand our emotions so we can calm down, focus, and be aware of the world around us!

The most important thing is to be aware of our needs so that we can make positive choices. Remember, we can always practice activities from the POP Chart at home, too, if we are ever having unpleasant feelings like when we're sad, anxious, or worried!

6

Implementation and Integration

The SEL practices are broken up into two chapters: SELF and SOCIAL. Please be mindful that students respond differently to movement and stillness depending on their mental and emotional needs as well as their exposure to trauma.

These practices are designed for universal, whole-class implementation (Tier I), facilitated by an educator, not only a social worker or counselor. Checking-in at the POP Chart should become part of the morning routine (during their non-instructional time). The teacher may also cue students to visit the POP Chart for a few minutes, during instructional time, or insert a practice during class to help positively shift student energy toward being present. For students with exceptionalities, offer extended time at the POP Chart and include activity modifications to promote inclusivity. Creating an accessible classroom environment is crucial for program implementation to be inclusive for all.

The activities are either written as extended scripts, which include classroom management cues and pacing suggestions, or are written simply as activities (often as sequences) to be read aloud by the teacher or implemented as directed. *Scripted material is in italic type throughout the book.*

As I have mentioned in other areas of this work, I am not a fan of scripted material being the main delivery vehicle for practitioners, as it does not build adult SEC or encourage reflection. The intention behind the design of the scripted activities is to give the educator a vehicle in which to learn the delivery, pacing, and classroom management style that best complements the content. Given the length, the scripts are **not** designed to be read aloud to the students. Instead, it is recommended the educator read through the scripts a few times to get a full picture of what the delivery looks, sounds, and feels like. Once the practitioner has mastered the pacing and classroom management cues, the POP Chart becomes a living, functioning element of the classroom, meeting both students' and teacher's needs throughout the school day.

Using the Agreements and building consensus around the practices is important, not just to build an emotionally and physically safe environment but also so the teacher can gain feedback from the students on their experiences. Each lesson contains a cue to discuss the "Why" behind the practices to build student agency and ownership of the strategies.

7

SELF (Intrapersonal) Practices

The practices within this chapter are designed to give students the space to cultivate SEC, namely Self-Awareness and Self-Regulation.

After each practice has been taught, it should be added to the POP Chart so that students can utilize it during their check-in routine or if they request a break during class.

The majority of the practices in this chapter are written as scripted lessons for educators. This is to help educators learn both new content and a new instructional style. These scripts are *written in italic type* for ease of implementation and are labeled **Educator Script** in bold at the top of the page.

To build practitioner competency, I highly suggest reading the scripted practices and reframing them in your own words. Be mindful of implicit bias when teaching the lesson and make the time to see all students through a culturally responsive and trauma-informed lens.

Too often, educators operate in silos. I strongly recommend sharing the practices that you feel are most successful with your students' parents or caregivers along with other educators and staff that work with your students. Continuity of approach, messaging, and practices between educators across the school community can greatly increase the positive impact on your students' SEC and overall well-being.

Yoga Sequence 1: Seated Arm Stretch and Starfish Pose

✓ **Educator Script**

Supplies:

◆ Sentence strip to add the activity to the POP Chart

Time: 5 minutes [poses may be done in isolation or as a sequence]

The Why Behind the Practice: *Today, we are practicing **yoga** poses. We can practice different yoga poses at school or home, any time we need a movement break. Movement breaks are healthy for our bodies and help us relax.*

Yoga is a practice where we move our bodies into different shapes or poses. Yoga connects the body and mind through movement and breathing. The most important thing when you practice yoga is to listen to your body. Notice when something feels good in your body and notice when something doesn't feel good in your body or hurts. Does anyone have any questions about yoga before we get started? We have time for three students to ask questions. [Educator responds to student questions.]

*Our first pose is **Seated Arm Stretch**. Hold the pose only as long as it feels good in your body.*

First: *Sit up tall in your seat.*

Then: *Raise your arms above your head.*

Next: *Stretch your arms up to the sky.*

Last: *Take five deep, slow breaths. When you are done, slowly lower your arms.*

Educator Tip: For movement in the classroom to be successful, it is vital that you articulate, model, and reinforce the concept of safe or personal space. For the physical and emotional safety of the classroom to be maintained, personal space should be taught and practiced in varying settings (i.e., lining up for dismissal, hallway behavior, lunch, recess, PE class, etc.) and by multiple stakeholders in the building all using common language around the concept. If a student's personal space is violated, you should pause the activity and re-teach Safe Space Bubble before continuing with the lesson.

Nicely done, everyone! Now we are going to try **Starfish Pose**.

When I say "Begin," please stand up and push in your chairs. [Educator cues students to push in their chairs.] *Please stand at least arms-width apart from your neighbor. Find your Safe Space Bubble so that you have plenty of room to move your body.* [In lieu of crowding the students all together on the rug, please use the "Scatter" technique to encourage students to honor their classmates' personal space.]

First: *Begin by standing with your feet apart, so your legs look like a triangle.*

Then: *Raise your arms above your head, like the letter "V." Now, your body should look like the letter "X."*

Next: *Push your feet down into the floor. Stretch both hands up to the sky.*

Last: *Take five deep, slow breaths. Yoga breathing is when you breathe quietly, deeply and slowly. We want to breathe quietly so that we do not disturb our neighbor. Nicely done, everyone! Remember to hold the pose only as long as feels good for your body. Once you begin to get tired, relax and find your breath.* [Educator slowly counts to 5.] *Nice job, everyone!*

Class, you all did an awesome job practicing yoga today. Well done! [Student name], *you did a very nice job managing your behavior during the activity and respecting your neighbor's personal space.* [Student name], *can you choose a volunteer to tell me the names of the two yoga poses we practiced together?* [Student names poses.] *That's right,* [Student name], *we learned* [educator says names aloud]. *I have made cards for these two poses and have added them to our POP Chart* [educator holds up sentence strips], *so that we can practice yoga any time we need a break or need to move our bodies.*

Yoga Sequence 2: Mountain Pose, Starfish Pose, and Seated Arm Stretch

✓ Educator Script

Supplies:

- Sentence strip to add the activity to the POP Chart

Time: 5 minutes [poses may be done in isolation or as a sequence]

The Why Behind the Practice: *Today, we are practicing **yoga** poses. We can practice different yoga poses at school or home, any time we need a movement break. Movement breaks are healthy for our bodies and help us relax if we are feeling worried or upset.*

Yoga is a practice. In this practice, we move our bodies into different shapes or poses. The two most important things when you practice yoga are to try your best and listen to your body. Does anyone have any questions about yoga before we get started? [Educator responds to student questions.]

When I say "Begin," please stand up and push in your chairs. [Educator cues students to push in their chairs.] *Please stand at least arms-width apart from your neighbor. Find your Safe Space Bubble so that you know you have plenty of room to move your body.* [In lieu of crowding the students all together on the rug, please use the "Scatter" technique] *It is important to keep our classroom safe by honoring our classmates' personal space.*

*Our first pose is **Mountain Pose**. Hold the pose only as long as it feels good for your body. Once you begin to get tired, relax your body and find your breath.*

First: *Stomp your feet.* [Educator models "stomp," "stomp."]

Then: *Stand up tall and proud.*

Last: *Take five slow, deep yoga breaths.* [Educator slowly counts to 5.]

Nicely done, class!

*Our second pose is **Starfish Pose**. Hold the pose only as long as feels good for your body. Once you begin to get tired, relax your body and find your breath.*

First: *Begin by standing with your feet apart, so your legs look like a triangle.*

Then: *Raise your arms above your head, like the letter "V." Now, your body should look like the letter "X."*

Next: *Push your feet down into the floor. Stretch both hands up to the sky.*

Last: *Take five deep, slow breaths. [Educator slowly counts to 5.] Nice job, everyone!*

Our next yoga pose is **Seated Arm Stretch**.

First: *Sit in your chair or on the floor with criss-cross applesauce legs.*

Then: *Raise your arms above your head, like the letter "V."*

Next: *Stretch both hands up to the sky.*

Last: *Take five deep, slow breaths. [Educator slowly counts to 5.] Nice job, everyone! When you are done, slowly lower your arms.*

[The educator will now choose a student demonstrating the classroom rules to lead the class through a quick pose review.] Let's take a moment to review the poses we practiced today. I am looking for a student who is demonstrating our classroom rules who can teach us one of the poses we learned today. [Educator chooses student. Student teaches a pose to the class while the educator counts to 5. Aides and paraprofessionals practice the pose along with the students.] Nicely done, Room [x]. Excellent work, everyone!

Now, may I have a volunteer to tell me the names of all three yoga poses we practiced together as a class? [Educator calls on student. Student names the three poses.] Great work, [Student name]! Together, we learned [educator names three poses and writes them on the board]. I have made cards for these poses and have added them to our POP Chart so that we can practice yoga any time we need a break, want to move our bodies, or are worried or sad. Yoga poses are also great if we need to cool down, focus, and be Ready to Learn.

Yoga Sequence 3: Mountain Pose, Tippy Toes Breath, and Tree Pose

✓ **Educator Script**

Supplies:

◆ Sentence strip to add the activity to the POP Chart

Time: 5 minutes [poses may be done in isolation or as a sequence]

The "Why" Behind the Practice: *Today, we are practicing **yoga** poses. We can practice different yoga poses at school or home, any time we need a movement break. Movement breaks are healthy for our bodies and help us relax if we are feeling worried or upset.*

Yoga is a practice. In this practice, we move our bodies into different shapes or poses. The two most important things when you practice yoga are to try your best and listen to your body. Does anyone have any questions about yoga before we get started? [Educator responds to student questions.]

When I say "Begin," please stand up and push in your chairs. [Educator cues students to push in their chairs.] *Please stand at least arms-width apart from your neighbor. Find your Safe Space Bubble so that you know you have plenty of room to move your body.* [In lieu of crowding the students all together on the rug, please use the "Scatter" technique.] *It is important to keep our classroom safe by honoring our classmates' personal space.*

*Our first pose is **Mountain Pose**. Hold the pose only as long as it feels good for your body. Once you begin to get tired, relax your body and find your breath.*

First: *Stomp your feet.* [Educator models "stomp," "stomp."]

Then: *Stand up tall and proud.*

Next: *Take five slow, deep yoga breaths.* [Educator slowly counts to 5.]

Nicely done, class!

*Our next pose will be **Tippy Toes Breath**. Before we begin, let's find our Safe Space Bubbles to help us respect our neighbor's personal space. Good job!*

First: *Stand up tall and proud.*

Then: *Look at something in front of you that is not moving, like a book.*

Next: *Slowly stand on your tiptoes.*

If you are having a hard time keeping your balance, don't hop around. To help you balance, place your hand on something next to you like a table or chair.

Last: *Let's take five deep yoga breaths together.* [Educator slowly counts to 5.]

Way to go, everyone!

Our last pose will be **Tree Pose**. *Before we begin, let's find our Safe Space Bubbles to help us respect our neighbor's personal space. Good job!*

First: *Stand up tall and proud.*

Then: *Lift one foot up, and turn it out to the side.* [Educator demonstrates and aides circulate around the room to assist students in finding this position.]

Next: *Place that foot above or below your knee.* [Educator demonstrates and aides circulate around the room to assist students in finding this position.] *To help you balance, look at something in front of you that is not moving, like a chair.*

Last: *Lift your arms overhead like the branches of a tree. Let's take five deep yoga breaths together.* [Educator slowly counts to 5.]

Nicely done, everyone!

Room [x], you all did an awesome job practicing yoga today. Well done! [Student name], you did a very nice job managing your behavior during the activity and respecting your neighbor's personal space. [Student name] can you choose a volunteer to tell me the names of the three yoga poses we practiced together as a class? [Educator calls on student. Student repeats poses.] *That's right, [Student name], we learned* [educator says names aloud]. *I have made cards for these poses and have added them to our POP Chart so that we can practice yoga any time we need a break or want to move our bodies. Yoga is a great tool to help us calm down, focus, and be ready to learn.*

Draw and Rip

✓ **Educator Script**

Supplies:

- Sentence strip to add the activity to the POP Chart
- Music
- Scrap paper
- Crayon, marker, or pencil
- Recycling bin or garbage can
- Clock or timer

Time: 10 minutes

The Why Behind the Practice: *Today, we are practicing **Draw and Rip**. We can practice Draw and Rip at school or home, any time we feel sad or something is bothering us. I have already created a card for Draw and Rip and added it to our POP Chart* [educator points to card]. *That way, we can practice Draw and Rip any time. This activity is a positive way to manage our emotions, and is also an easy thing to do if we are at home and need a break.*

[The aides and paraprofessionals circulate around the room to make sure every student has scratch paper and a crayon, marker, or pencil before they begin.]

To begin, pause for a moment and close your eyes. Or, if closing your eyes doesn't feel OK today, pick something to focus on, like a picture on the bulletin board. Let's all take a few deep yoga breaths together [educator models]. *Is there anything that is making you sad or worried today?*

We're going to practice Draw and Rip by drawing our worries on a piece of paper, then ripping it up and tossing it into the recycle bin. I am going to set the time for 2 minutes. When the 2 minutes is over, we will all rip up our papers and toss our worries into the recycling bin. [Educator moves the recycling bin to the center of the room.] *Tossing our worries into the recycling bin helps us focus and be ready to learn. No one will see what you draw, even me. All our papers are ripped up and placed in the recycling bin.*

Once we have finished ripping up our papers, I will place the recycle bin behind my desk. I am now setting the timer for 2 minutes. Begin drawing your worries.

[Adults also participate in the activity to model for students that they also have worries and that Draw and Rip is an appropriate strategy for dealing with unpleasant emotions. The educator prompts the students by table to walk up to the recycle bin to rip and toss their papers. Once the last group is done, the educator places the recycle bin behind their desk so that the students are reassured that the contents of the bin will not be tampered with.]

Great job, Room [x]! We all learned a new practice to help us when we feel worried or sad. I also saw students making positive choices about their behavior. [Student name], you did an excellent job managing your behavior during the activity and respecting your neighbor's personal space. Can you please place this card for Draw and Rip in our POP Chart? [Student walks to POP Chart, adds sentence strip to the pocket chart.] *We can practice Draw and Rip at home or school, any time we feel worried.*

While [Student name] is adding Draw and Rip to our POP Chart, we have time for [x number of] students to share how their bodies are feeling **after** *Draw and Rip. Do we feel relaxed? Do we feel calm? Would anyone like to share with our class today?* [Educator calls on students to share.]

Listening Breath

✓ **Educator Script**

Supplies:

◆ Sentence strip to add the activity to the POP Chart

Time: 3 minutes

The Why Behind the Practice: *Today, we are practicing* **Listening Breath**. *We can practice Listening Breath at school or home, any time we feel sad or something is bothering us.*

I have already created a card for Listening Breath and added it to our POP Chart [educator points to card]. *That way, we can practice Listening Breath anytime. This activity is a positive way to manage our emotions, and is also an easy thing to do if we are at home and need a break.*

To begin, pause for a moment and close your eyes. Or, if closing your eyes doesn't feel OK today, pick something to focus on, like a picture on the bulletin board. Let's all take a few deep yoga breaths together [educator models]. *How is your energy today? Are you tired? Are you excited? Do you have a lot of energy and it is hard to focus?*

> **Educator Tip**: For students with exceptionalities or those who may have experienced trauma, sitting with their eyes closed can feel unsafe. Always provide an alternative, like picking a spot to focus on in front of them.

First: *Listen to the sounds around you. What do you hear?* [Educator gives examples of sounds: *Voices in the hallway? Cars outside the window?*] *Choose one sound and try to listen to only that sound.*

Then: *Pay attention to that sound. Breathe in and breathe out for the next five breaths.* [Educator slowly counts to 5.] *Now, let's listen to the soft, quiet sound of our own breathing. Let's be really quiet and try to listen our breathing, tune out everything else.* [Educator models]

Last: *How are you feeling? Do you feel relaxed, focused, and ready to learn? The next time you are having a difficult time focusing in class or controlling your behavior, take a moment to listen to the sounds around you or to the sound of your own breathing.*

Happy Note

Supplies:

- Sentence strip to add the activity to the POP Chart
- Paper
- Crayons, markers, or pencil

Time: 4 minutes

The Why Behind the Practice: Today, we are drawing a **Happy Note**. This activity is a creative way to support ourselves when we are feeling sad or scared.

I have already created a card for Happy Note and added it to our POP Chart [educator points to card]. That way, we can practice it whenever we like. This activity is a positive way to manage our emotions, and is also an easy thing to do if we are at home and need a happy boost.

First: Pass out a small sheet of paper and crayons to each student.

Then: Before they begin drawing, they find their breath and check-in. What do they need to remember to be strong in a tough situation today?

Next: The students draw themselves a note to keep with them throughout the day. The note can be a confidence boost or a gentle reminder. The note can have a picture of their favorite animal, fruit, or something that makes them feel happy.

Last: Cue the students to take out their note when they need a quick boost.

> **Educator Tip**: This activity is great for students who go home to challenging domestic situations.

Memory Minute

Supplies:

- Sentence strip to add the activity to the POP Chart
- Timer

Time: 5 minutes

The Why Behind the Practice: *Today, we are practicing **Memory Minute**. We can practice Memory Minute at school or home, any time we need a break. Breaks are healthy for our minds and help us relax.*

First: Make sure your room is quiet and that all screens (smartboards, tablets, etc.) are turned off or not visible. Cue your students to stretch their arms to the sky to find their Safe Space Bubbles so that they can respect their neighbor's personal space and will not be a distraction to themselves or others.

Then: Hold up a white sheet of paper. Ask your students to close their eyes, if they feel comfortable, and visualize the white sheet of paper in their minds (remember to offer the trauma-informed choice to leave the eyes open).

Next: Set the timer for 30 seconds and ask your students to remain quiet. (Once your students have practiced the activity for a few weeks, feel free to increase the time by 10-second intervals until you reach a minute.) Ask your students to keep their voices and bodies quiet, thinking only of the white sheet of paper. For 30 seconds everyone, including the adults in the room, are quiet and focused. No screens, no distractions. (Let's remember, this is an important well-being break for the educators as well!)

Last: When the 30 seconds has concluded, gently cue your students to open their eyes if they were closed, or to bring their focus back to the front of the room.

> **Educator Tip**: To cultivate student Self-Awareness, engage your class in a discussion of how this activity felt. Do they feel relaxed and calm after the practice? Was 30 seconds too long/short? How do their bodies feel after the activity?

Tap Our Worries Away

Supplies:

◆ Sentence strip to add the activity to the POP Chart

Time: 5 minutes

The Why Behind the Practice: *Today, we are practicing **Tap Our Worries Away**. We can practice Tap Our Worries Away at school or home, any time we are feeling worried or nervous.*

First: Make sure your room is quiet and that all screens (smartboards, tablets, etc.) are turned off or not visible. Cue your students to stretch their arms to the sky to find their Safe Space Bubbles so that they can respect their neighbor's personal space and will not be a distraction to themselves or others.

Then: To demonstrate Tap Your Worries Away for your students, make two fists hold them up in front of your chest. Now, raise your pointer fingers to make the number 1. Bring them together to touch, (like a little triangle). Cue your students to do the same.

Next: Ask your students to take a few deep breaths and picture something that is making them nervous or worried.

Last: Ask your students to tap their index fingers together as you softly say in unison "Tap, tap, tap. Tap, tap, tap. Tap your worries away." (Repeat three times.) When the practice has concluded, gently cue your students to lower their hands and notice how they are feeling.

> **Educator Tip**: To cultivate student Self-Awareness, engage your class in a discussion of how this activity felt. Do they feel relaxed and calm after the practice? Do they feel less worried or nervous? How could they practice this activity at home or any time they feel worried?

Cotton Ball Breath

Supplies:

- Sentence strip to add the activity to the POP Chart
- Bag of cotton balls and/or small pieces of scrap paper
- Timer

Time: 5 minutes

The Why Behind the Practice: *Today, we are practicing* **Cotton Ball Breath** *to help us learn about how the breath moves in and out of our bodies. Cotton Ball Breath builds our body awareness by teaching us about how we breathe.*

First: Pass out one cotton ball per student. If students do not like the touch of cotton, a small, wadded-up piece of scrap paper may be used instead.

Then: Each student places the cotton ball in the palm of one hand and places the other hand on the table. Remind students to keep their feet flat on the floor and their bottoms in their seats.

Next: Ask your students to blow the cotton ball from the palms of their hands to their fingers, without it falling onto the table.

Last: Continue for 60 seconds. Cue your students to continuously slow their breath down so the cotton ball moves slowly in their hands. (For example, *If we breath out or exhale powerfully, the cotton ball travels too far. If we use a soft exhalation, or softly breathe out, the cotton ball doesn't move enough. How can we find a breath that is just right?*)

Educator Tip: This is an excellent practice when students' energy is high, as it helps learners relax the body by focusing on the breath. This practice is great for a student who is struggling with behavior and needs to pause for a moment. To cultivate student body awareness, engage your class in a discussion of how this activity felt. Did they feel it was simple or challenging? Do they feel relaxed and calm after the practice? What did they learn about their breathing?

Equal Breath

Supplies:

- Sentence strip to add the activity to the POP Chart

Time: 3 minutes

The Why Behind the Practice: *Today, we are practicing **Equal Breath**. We can practice Equal Breath when we are feeling wiggly and it is difficult to stay in our seats, or if we are feeling worried or scared. This activity is also great to practice at home, if we need a moment to cool down. I have already created a card for Equal Breath and added it to our POP Chart [educator points to card]. That way, we can practice it whenever we like.*

First: *Begin seated and place your feet flat on the floor, roll your shoulders back, and lengthen your spine.*

Then: *Notice the pattern of your breath. Notice your inhalations, or deep breaths in, and your exhalations, or deep breaths out. Which is longer? Which is shorter?*

Next: *With your next breath, make your inhalation and exhalation the same length. Let's start with the count of 4. Slowly count to 4 as you inhale. [Educator slowly counts aloud.] 1-2-3-4. Now, also count to 4 as you exhale. The exercise is to match the length of your breath in, or inhalation, with your breath out, or exhalation. Breathe in for the count of 4. [Educator slowly counts aloud.] 1-2-3-4. Breathe out for the count of 4. [Educator slowly counts aloud.] 1-2-3-4.*

Last: *Continue breathing this way for several minutes. You may experiment with changing the number you count to; just breathe slowly and relax.*

> **Educator Tip**: Visibly count along on your fingers to help students keep the pace of the activity.

Lion's Breath

✓ Educator Script

Supplies:

- Sentence strip to add the activity to the POP Chart

Time: 5 minutes

The Why Behind the Practice: *Today, we are practicing* **Lion's Breath**. *We can practice Lion's Breath at school or home, any time we feel angry or something is bothering us. We can practice Lion's Breath whenever we need to. This activity is a positive way to manage our emotions, and is also an easy thing to do if we are at home and need a break.*

To begin, pause for a moment and close your eyes. Or, if closing your eyes doesn't feel OK today, pick something to focus on, like a picture on the bulletin board. Let's all take a few deep yoga breaths together [educator models]. *Is there anything that is making you sad or worried today? Is there a part of your body that hurts or feels achy? Perhaps your stomach hurts or you have headache?* [Educator can and should customize this language to fit the needs of classroom.] *When we practice Lion's Breath, we breathe calming, cooling breaths to the parts of our bodies that need to relax.*

We are going to breathe like lions by taking a deep breath in and exhaling a strong breath out [educator and aides demonstrate]. *Lions are strong animals. Sometimes, being strong is taking a moment to stop and listen to your body. If our bodies are worried, it is important to find a practice to help us feel better.*

Room [x], do we see any potential problems with practicing Lion's Breath, like students giggling while we are all trying to breathe? [Educator calls on one or two students to discuss potential pitfalls.]

Thank you, [Student names]. How can we help each other if these problems happen? [Educator discusses problem solving with students.]

Thank you, Room [x], for sharing your thoughts respectfully and thoughtfully. I witnessed students actively listening to their peers. Well done! Now, let's begin Lion's Breath!

First: *Sit up with your back tall. Close your eyes, or pick a spot to look at in front of you.*

Next: *Take a deep breath and open your mouth wide. Say "AHHHHHH!"* [Educator models.]

> **Educator Tip**: Students should not "roar" or be overly loud at this time. You may need to stop the activity, restate the expectations, and begin again.

Last: *Let's repeat Lion's Breath three more times together. This time, let's be quiet lions. Let's breathe out anything that may be bothering us so we can focus and be ready to learn in class today.*

Well done, Room [x]. I am impressed! I saw students making positive decisions about their behavior and being quiet lions. Thank you!

[Student name], you did an excellent job managing your behavior during the activity. Can you please add the card for Lion's Breath to our POP Chart? [Student walks to POP Chart, adds sentence strip to the pocket chart.]

Now, our class has another strategy to help us be ready to learn any time we are stressed or anxious. Remember, Room [x], we can also practice Lion's Breath at home or school, any time we feel stress in our bodies.

While [Student name] is adding Lion's Breath to our POP Chart, we have time for [x number of] students to share their emotions and feelings with a one-word check-in.

I am looking for students who would like to share one word about how they are feeling after practicing Lion's Breath with our class. [Educator calls on students to share one word such as "relaxed" or "calm."]

8

SOCIAL (Interpersonal) Practices

These practices are designed to give students the space to cultivate awareness of themselves within a group, or Social Awareness, and how their mood, energy, and emotions impact the group as a whole.

After each activity has been taught, it should be added to the POP Chart so that students have a visual reminder of practices available to them to regulate and manage emotions.

Many of the practices in this chapter are written as scripted lessons for educators. This is to help educators learn both new content and a new instructional style. These scripts are *written in italic type* for ease of implementation and are labeled **Educator Script** in bold at the top of the page.

To build practitioner competency, I highly suggest reading the scripted activities and reframing them in your own words. Be mindful of implicit bias when teaching the lesson and make the time to see all students through a trauma-informed lens.

Too often, educators operate in silos. I strongly recommend sharing the practices that you feel are most successful with your students' parents or caregivers along with other educators and staff that work with your students. Continuity of approach, messaging, and practices between educators across the school community can greatly increase the positive impact on your students' SEC and overall well-being.

Color Breath

✓ Educator Script

Supplies:

- Sentence strip to add the activity to the POP Chart

Time: 5 minutes

The Why Behind the Practice: *Today, we are practicing **Color Breath** to help us learn about how the breath moves in and out of our bodies. Color Breath builds our body awareness by teaching us about our breathing. This activity also gives us an opportunity to learn about our classmates and their favorite colors.*

First: *Sit up tall and proud in your seat.*

Then: *I will choose a student who has demonstrated our classroom rules today to pick their favorite color.* [Select a student and have them share their favorite color.]

Next: *Let's all take a deep breath and close our eyes.*

Last: *Exhaling together, let's chant the color chosen. (For example: "Grrreeeeeeeeeeennn.")* [Teacher and aides model, assisting students who need help. Please note: multisyllabic words will need to be modeled for the class ahead of time. For instance, lavender becomes Illllaaaaa-veeeeennnn-ddddeeeerrr. Or, encourage students to choose a monosyllabic color like red, green, blue, gold, white, black, gray, pink, tan, teal, or brown.]

Bee's Breath

✓ Educator Script

Supplies:

- Sentence strip to add the activity to the POP Chart

Time: 5 minutes

The Why Behind the Practice: *Today, we are practicing **Bee's Breath** to help us learn about how the breath moves in and out of our bodies. Bee's Breath builds our body awareness by teaching us about our breathing. This activity also helps us calm down if our bodies are wiggly and we need to focus.*

First: *Sit at your desk with your shoulders rolled back and your feet flat on the floor.*

Then: *Close your eyes or pick a spot to focus on, like a letter on our bulletin board. If it feels comfortable, put your hands over your ears.*

Next: *Take a deep breath. Exhaling to the count of 4, make a buzzing sound like a bee.* [Teacher and aides model, assisting students who need help.]

Last: *Keep your eyes closed and let's repeat Bee's Breath four times together.*

Educator Tip: For students with exceptionalities, hands over the ears may not be possible. Instead, give students a "fidget" or squeeze ball to focus their gaze on during the activity.

Positive Paperchain

Supplies:

- Sentence strip to add the activity to the POP Chart
- Staplers or masking tape
- Multicolored strips of construction paper
- Crayon or pencils

Time: 10 minutes

The Why Behind the Practice: *Today, we are creating a **Positive Paperchain** to help us be proud of our classroom community. Taking the time to create a Positive Paperchain together helps us appreciate who we are and the awesome things about our classroom. When we see our paperchain hanging in class we can breathe in feelings of positivity and pride.*

Read the directions aloud while your students follow along. Depending on the age level of your students, teachers and aides should be on hand to help students assemble the paperchain.

First: Ask your students to take a deep breath and think of a reason they are proud of their classroom community (such as being active listeners, being good friends, or working well with others).

Then: Instruct your students to draw (or write) their favorite thing about their class on their strip of construction paper.

Next: Cue your students to share what they drew (or wrote) with the students next to them, using the words, "I drew two kids playing because . . ."

Last: Ask a few student leaders to collect all the pieces of paper. Working with an aide or other adult, staple and create the colorful paperchain. Once the chain is complete, cue your students to breathe in feelings of positivity and pride.

Educator Tip: Grow the paperchain around the room all year. It is a great visual reminder of the positive energy that the classroom community has shared. As the teacher, feel free to add to the paperchain at any point throughout the week when you observe something positive in your classroom: "I received a wonderful report from our sub yesterday. Thank you, Room 105! I am going to add a positive thought to our paperchain!" Celebrating positivity and owning your strengths are great practices to model for your students.

Compliment Partners

Supplies:

- ◆ Sentence strip to add the activity to the POP Chart
- ◆ Clock or timer

Time: 5 minutes

The Why Behind the Practice: *Today, we are playing* **Compliment Partners***! A compliment is when you say something kind about someone else. Compliment Partners is a great way to use kind words to build our classroom community. This activity also helps us stay healthy by getting us up and out of our seats to take a movement break.*

First: Play music and ask your students to move around the room [walking feet, tiptoe feet, etc.]. When the music stops, cue your students to find a partner that is closest to them. Ask your students to stand facing their classmate, about arms-length apart.

Then: Announce which student in the pair will go first (the student standing closest to the door, etc.). Allow each student about 30–45 seconds to compliment their partner by remembering a time they were being kind, caring, a good friend, good at sharing, etc. (Cue the partners to switch once their time is up.)

Next: Before the music begins again and your students find new partners, ask your students to *hug or gently high-five their partners to show respect for the compliment they shared*. Continue the activity for at least two more rounds, time permitting.

Last: To close the activity, ask your students to return to their seats or the rug. Ask your students to sit up tall, shoulders rolled back, and eyes closed, and take five deep breaths. Cue them to think about all the kind words that they heard and they shared. (This last phase of the activity is crucial to counter any negative self-talk that our students may hear at home. If time permits, ask your students to share with the class and record keywords on the board.)

> **Educator Tip**: For this activity to be successful, it is important you appropriately frame the experience by discussing the difference between a true, observational compliment and a joke or self-deprecating comment. A true compliment would be "You are a good friend and always help me when I am in need." Instead of, "You are a good friend today, but yesterday you were annoying me on the playground."

Pass the Animal

Supplies:

- ◆ Sentence strip to add the activity to the POP Chart
- ◆ Stuffed animal

Time: 10 minutes

The Why Behind the Practice: *Today, we are playing* **Pass the Animal***! Pass the Animal is a great way to work on building our classroom community. This activity also helps us stay healthy by getting us up and out of our seats to take a movement break.*

First: Arrange your students in one large circle, about arms-width apart, respecting their neighbor's personal space by finding their Safe Space Bubbles.

Then: Choose a student to begin the activity by turning to the student to their left, making eye contact, smiling, and gently passing them the stuffed animal. (It is important to engage in trauma-informed practices here, making the eye contact optional for those students who feel uncomfortable.)

Next: The student who received the stuffed animal now turns to the student on their left, makes eye contact, smiles, and passes them the stuffed animal. This continues until each student has had a turn.

Last: After the stuffed animal has successfully made it around the circle once, the teacher closes the circle with, "Thank you."

> **Educator Tip**: Modify this activity to learn students' names by moving around the circle saying the name of the student that receives the stuffed animal. For instance, the student on my right passes me the stuffed animal, so the whole group says "Carla." Then, I pass the animal to the student on my left and the whole group says, "Dottie," then on to "Remi," etc. This is a fantastic way to not only learn students' names but also to learn how to pronounce them correctly.

Kind Kid Postcard

✓ **Educator Script**

Supplies:

- Sentence strip to add the activity to the POP Chart
- Index cards, 1 per student
- Postage stamps (optional)
- Pens and pencils

Time: 7 minutes

The Why Behind the Practice: *Today, we are creating **Kind Kid Postcards** to celebrate what kind kids we are! This activity reminds us to find our voices and notice when we are kind and compassionate toward ourselves and others.*

To begin, distribute index cards to your students. Then, read the directions aloud while your students follow along.

First: *Take a deep breath and think of a reason you are proud of yourself such as being a kind friend, or a good group leader.*

Then: *On the front of the index card (the side without lines), draw a picture of why you are proud of yourself today.*

Next: *Write your name on the back of the postcard (the side with lines).*

Last: *I will help you address your postcard to someone with whom you would like to share your positive thoughts such as your parent/caregiver, principal, or art/music/PE teacher.*

Educator Tip: Once the postcards are complete, you can save postage by distributing the school-bound postcards to your colleagues' mailboxes after school. For students with exceptionalities, photocopy a template with a space for students to draw and a line to write their names. Draw a sample on the board for your students to reference.

Community-Based Service Learning Project

Supplies:

◆ To be determined based upon project chosen

Estimated Project Time: 3–4 weeks

The Why Behind the Practice: *We are planning and participating in a* **Community-Based Service Learning Project** *to connect with and give back to our community. In Social Emotional Learning this year we have worked hard to develop our leadership, and teamwork skills. We have worked on being the solution and on using our voices. Now, we will create a Service Learning Project to step into action and be the solution for folx in our school.*

Service Learning Project: Having students work collaboratively to create a Service Learning Project is the perfect way to reinforce a sense of community. Service Learning Projects are most successful when they bring different groups together—for example: one classroom partnering with an older to plan a school green space or draw pictures for the local senior center.

Prior to the start of the project, it is important to message the concept of responsible giving and/or *giving back* to the community. Instead of framing the Service Learning Project as a one-sided proposition of *us* helping *them*, discuss the ways in which *giving back* to the community creates an opportunity for the class to contemplate their role within the community, to share their voices with community members, to collaborate in the creation of something meaningful and relevant, and to engage in a relationship of reciprocal learning. It is also crucial that the students set goals around the project, measure its impact, and examine prospects for sustainability, thus moving away from one-off monetary gifts and instead developing positive youth identity by being the solution and giving back via time and human connection.

> **Educator Tip:** Some states, such as Illinois, have Service Learning Standards that connect nicely to their Social Emotional Learning standards (in this case, most notably, "Goal 3—Demonstrate decision-making skills and responsible behaviors in personal, school, and community contexts"). Connecting these standards can be a great way to create metrics to measure the overall impact of the project. This project is also an excellent opportunity to build bridges between students with different access needs!

9

Crafting SEL Stories

The SEL story is an instrumental element of any educator's approach to SEL. It is not only the reading of the story or the theme of the story itself, it is the peer-to-peer communication tools employed during the activity that are the richest and most impactful aspect.

Here are two examples of how to implement SEL stories in your classroom:

Teams: The students work in small teams to decide on a solution to a problem or issue.

Classroom Conversation: A dialogue lead by the teacher, using a template or story provided.

The educator may choose to use one of the templates provided to create a culturally relevant SEL story based upon problems or issues the class is experiencing. Or, the educator may choose to read one of the scripted SEL stories provided and facilitate a thoughtful dialogue with the students.

Before choosing which option will work best, reflect on happenings in the school community and the interpersonal needs of your students. What would best serve them at present? Look at the time available for your lesson, as the pacing of the activity is important to build reflective potency.

As the educator delivering the lesson, reflect on your own SEC around the topic. What lessons have you learned that you can share with your students? What are your current challenges and areas of growth around the topic? Can you own those for your students? ("Even though I am a teacher, I struggle with Self-Awareness sometimes, too. This past weekend, I rolled my eyes when . . .")

Implementation steps for delivering SEL stories are outlined here. Some of the SEL terminology embedded in the sample stories is shown in **bold** to make it easy to emphasize during instruction. Cultural relevancy is key for SEL to take root in students' lives. The terminology should be used as part of a common classroom language during SEL instruction and should be reinforced throughout the day.

Delivery of SEL Stories

Step 1: Look at the POP Chart. Where did the majority of students place their magnets at your last check-in? Reflect on or inquire about what is happening in their/your community and in our country. Which emotions or feelings are most represented in your class today and what do your students most need?

Step 2: Choose the SEL story format:
Option A: Teams
Option B: Classroom Conversation

Step 3: Close the practice with a Memory Minute to give your students an opportunity to reflect on what was shared before moving onto their next activity.

Messaging the Why

The following text in italic type is a scripted lesson for introducing the SEL stories to your students. As with the other scripted lessons in this book, it is not recommended that you read the script aloud word-for-word, as that would not help develop your competency as a practitioner. Instead, the script is meant to provide a solid idea of how the content is framed, paced, and managed. Read the script a few times, take notes, and then make it your own.

Today we are going to be sharing stories about Social Emotional Learning (SEL). When big things are happening at school or in our community, we will talk about them together using our SEL stories. These stories are a great way to work together to find solutions to tough problems, to talk about emotions that we are curious about, and to discuss things that might be making us feel sad, worried, or scared.

Option A: Teams

The Why Behind the Practice: *Today, we will be working together and using our imaginations to come up with an answer to [x problem or question]. By working together we are using our voices to solve problems. Let's remember what we have learned using our POP Chart. Before we get started, let's all take a breath together so we can focus our bodies and minds!* [Educator leads class through a deep breath.]

First: Write the problem or question on the board, like "How can our class do a better job sharing the soccer balls at recess so everyone gets a turn?" Or, "What do we do if we are worried that someone we know is really sick?"

Then: Place students in groups of four or five and set the timer for 4 minutes. When you say "Begin," the students will share their ideas on what is the best solution to the problem. [Educator should pre-teach/re-teach what active listening looks, sounds, and feels like to help students be successful. This is also a great time to use the Talking Stick!]

Next: At the end of the 4 minutes, the educator calls on one student from each group to share what ideas their group discussed. [Educator writes the ideas on the board.]

Last: Once each group has shared, the educator chooses one student to lead the class through a deep, relaxing breath.

In order for this exercise to have impact, students must feel the activity was relevant to their lives and has an effect on their immediate circumstances. Besides the major benefits of tailor-making relevant SEL content for your classroom, the speaking and listening inherent in this activity are great for building interpersonal relationships among students.

This is an excellent activity for helping students take ownership of their behavior, both as individuals and as a class, and to find solutions in real time. For instance, if your students misbehave at an assembly, when you return to your classroom, put the students in their teams and have them discuss a solution. This not only helps students develop a sense of personal responsibility but it also helps them see the impact of their actions, both positive and negative, on the classroom community.

> **Educator Tip**: Keep an on-going list of competencies, like Self-Awareness, that your class is practicing. Also, this is a wonderful opportunity to build consensus around a solution that you would like to add to your classroom Agreements!

Option B: Classroom Conversations

Use the template here to write SEL stories for your students. Be sure to take the time to cultivate cultural awareness and examine any implicit bias that may arise for you when engaging in this activity. Building these skills in yourself will show your students that you care about what is important to them. Sample reflection questions are also provided to conclude each lesson. In case you are having a difficult time getting started, I have included six sample SEL stories later in the chapter.

Template 1
_____ (name) is on the playground and is in a difficult situation. They _____ (name difficult situation). Because they were upset, _____ (name) did _____ (negative action), which is not a positive step toward a solution. How can _____ (name) use one of the activities in the POP Chart to make a more positive choice the next time? What is an example of a more positive choice in this situation?

Template 2
Over the weekend, _____ (name) got into trouble at their grandma's house. They know that it is their job to fix what happened. But they lied, which only made the situation worse. Now _____ (name) does not know how to make it better. What is a positive way for _____ (name) to own their behavior and fix the problem? Is there a cool down activity from our POP Chart could that help them pause and make a more positive choice if they are in this situation again?

Template 3
Room _____ misbehaved today in _____. Their teacher is disappointed because she knows that if they had stayed calm and focused, Room _____ could have made more positive choices about their behavior. To do better next time, Room _____ needs to think about what happened and decide what to do next. What are two things that Room _____ could do to stay calm and focused next time?

Sample SEL Stories

SEL words are shown in **bold** for the educator to reinforce throughout the day during instruction, add to their SEL word walls, or include in correspondence home to parents and caregivers.

1. Violet was **upset** with three kids in her class who were always misbehaving during snack time. If Violet's class continued to **behave poorly** their class party was going to be taken away. Violet was afraid that these three kids were going to ruin it for everyone else. One day, Violet got really frustrated and yelled at the three students to "BE QUIET!"

May I have a volunteer to tell me what happens in the story? [Educator asks one student to explain the story.]

*Now, may I have two volunteers to explain which practices, like breathing or yoga, from the POP Chart Violet could have used to help her calm **her anger** with her classmates and **express her feelings** without yelling?* [Educator asks two students to connect the SEL story to the activities in the POP Chart. Once the students conclude, the educator closes the activity by rephrasing their explanations in one or two sentences.]

2. Patrick came home from school upset because a friend of his wasn't nice to him on the playground. He knew from the **heavy feeling in his stomach and the tightness in his chest** that he was **holding a lot of hurt feelings in his body**. He knew he could make himself feel better if he paused to take a few deep breaths.

May I have a volunteer to tell me what happens in the story? [Educator asks one student to explain the story.]

Now, may I have two volunteers to explain which practices, like breathing or yoga, Patrick can use to help him notice how he's feeling and what's happening in his body? [Educator asks two students to connect the SEL story to the activities in the POP Chart. Once the students conclude, the educator closes the activity by rephrasing their explanations in one or two sentences.]

3. Shakita left her favorite teddy bear at her dad's apartment. Shakita did not have her teddy bear and she missed Show and Tell at school the next day. She was very **angry with herself**. Shakita knows that she needs to **control her emotions** and be **kind to herself**, but she doesn't quite know how.

May I have a volunteer to tell me what happens in the story? [Educator asks one student to explain the story.]

*Now, may I have two volunteers to explain which practices, like breathing or yoga, Shakita can use to help her with **her anger and frustration?*** [Educator asks two students to connect the SEL story to the activities in the POP Chart. Once the students conclude, the educator closes the activity by rephrasing their explanations in one or two sentences.]

4. Precious doesn't think she can draw very well. Whenever she runs into a problem with one of her drawings or paintings, she **gives up** because she thinks it is too hard. Precious was chosen by the principal to paint a picture for the art show. She was worried her picture

wouldn't be good. She **wanted to give up**, but she always **tried her best**. When the art show was over, Precious was proud of herself.

May I have a volunteer to tell me what happens in the story? [Educator asks one student to explain the story.]

Now, may I have two volunteers to explain which practices, like breathing or yoga, Precious can use to help the next time she feels worried or feels like she wants to give up? [Educator asks two students to connect the SEL story to the activities in the POP Chart. Once the students conclude, the educator closes the activity by rephrasing their explanations in one or two sentences.]

5. LeAndra and Terry are sitting in a circle with their classmates. Terry is sitting very close to LeAndra and he is playing with her hair. LeAndra is **uncomfortable** and feels her **Safe Space Bubble is being violated**. It is important that Terry **respects his neighbor's personal space**. LeAndra asked Terry, "Can you please scoot over and stop touching my hair?" Terry apologized and moved a few inches away. LeAndra responded by saying, "Thank you for apologizing. Please do not do it again."

May I have a volunteer to tell me what happens in the story? [Educator asks one student to explain the story.]

May I have two volunteers explain to me how LeAndra used her words to say what she needed to feel comfortable? [Educator asks two students to connect the SEL story to the activities in the POP Chart. Once the students conclude, the teacher closes the activity by rephrasing their explanations in one or two sentences. The educator also notes that LeAndra did not say "It is OK" when Terry apologized. She accepted his apology and created a clear boundary for next time.]

6. Sometimes in school, Martin gets **angry** when he has his hand up and the teacher calls on another student. Martin knows he is getting **frustrated** because he can feel his ears getting red and his cheeks burning. But instead of blurting out the answer or rolling his eyes, he **takes a breath** and waits to raise his hand until the next question. Sometimes the teacher will call on him, and sometimes, because the class is so big, he doesn't get a turn.

May I have a volunteer to tell me what happens in the story? [Educator asks one student to explain the story.]

Now, may I have two volunteers to explain which activities Martin can use to help him with his frustration? [Educator asks two students to connect the SEL story to the activities in the POP Chart. Once the students conclude, the educator closes the activity by rephrasing their explanations in one or two sentences.]

10

Recruiting Your Administrator

For years, schools have looked at SEL as a quick fix or a crisis intervention. We have presupposed Adult SEC, yet have also underestimated paraprofessionals, non-certified, and classified staff by making the delivery of SEL lessons exclusively the responsibility of either classroom teachers or social workers.

When we remember that SEL is a process, an approach, a practice over time and not a linear curriculum or *lessons* that students master, we are able to do what we do best, forge deep and meaningful connections with our students. Give students the space to get to know themselves, and give us the time to get to know them.

For many of us, human connection is what called us to education. If we take care of our SEC and well-being, then we can be emotionally available to others and connect with our colleagues and students more authentically.

Time is our greatest commodity. How we use our time reflects what we prioritize both personally and professionally. Yet, due to the constraints of the current educational system, many of us have little influence on how we spend our time with students.

In closing, I have included a little note for your administrators. Next time you walk by their office, pass them a copy of these pages. Or, borrow a few lines and pop them in an email. In visiting schools across the globe, and having been a curriculum coordinator myself, I know that administrators absolutely want to do right by their educators. Many are simply juggling too many priorities to stop and ask, "How can I help?"

Let's help our administrators by telling them what we need to practice SEL: time and clarity of purpose.

A Note to Administrators

Want to make SEL more impactful in your school or district? Want to help your teachers make more meaningful human connections with your students? Begin with Adult SEL and well-being. Make time. *Real* time. Focus only on well-being for the first months, no deliverables attached. The tough work is to quell the concerns of the naysayers. SEL, mindfulness, and well-being can be built into the district or school's culture across disciplines in a way that is equitable and anti-racist, as long as *you* make time in the schedule and you let your team know why they are doing it.

This can be a challenge, as SEL or mindfulness often can be seen as a separate add-on that requires little or no integration or proficiency on the part of the educator delivering the instruction. Being able to guide students to understand their feelings and emotions in a trauma-informed and culturally responsive way requires educators to deeply examine their implicit biases and engage in continual race and identity development work, which can seem insurmountable in a school setting. Without culturally responsive integration or practitioner competency, the benefits of SEL can be limited and short term, at best. SEL and mindfulness are best implemented when they are integrated into the climate and culture not just of the classroom but of the larger school and district.

When I finished my teaching certification in 2000, I left school having seen the term *Social Emotional Learning* included on only one professor's syllabus. Mindfulness was absent all together. Many of the teachers I coach (from urban Chicago to hilly New Hampshire to rural Oklahoma) had a similar pre-service experience.

So, while the movement to include SEL and mindfulness in schools continues to gain momentum, as educators we find ourselves in a difficult spot. We have adopted state standards for SEL content that many of our teachers are not competent to deliver due to a lack of training. To complicate the matter, they may be unaware of the gaps in their efficacy and juggling many responsibilities with little time or resources to grow their skill set. In many schools I have worked with, stakeholders are utilizing effective SEL tools across the building, but nothing has been codified. While there may be wonderful SEL and mindfulness practices taking place, there is no common language and students spend the bulk of their time engaging in a form of SEL code-switching from room to room, instead of being present in their practice. SEL may be called "SEL" in a student's classroom and then "Cool Down" when they go to see the dean, a "Wellness Break" when they get to their PE class, and then "Relaxation Time" when they are working with the social worker. While each of these stakeholders is well intentioned and, most likely, implementing solid practices, the students spend their time decoding what is happening in which setting instead of embodying the practices themselves. This is why high-quality professional learning opportunities are so important: they create common language, alignment, and practices across the school building. But, they must be coupled with clear messaging and expectations from you as to why we are doing this work and who is expected to do what.

Most importantly, be very clear about how much time should be devoted to SEL. Do not talk vaguely about priorities. Give specific amounts of time you expect adults in your building to devote to both non-instructional SEL skill-building (intentional, interpersonal relationships between adults and students) and instructional SEL skill-building (teaching SE competencies, embedding SEL into academic content, etc.) each day. Draw a line in the sand, stick to it, and evaluate folx on whether or not they do it. Then, provide every caring adult in your building, including paraprofessionals and non-certified staff, the training they need to be successful. Remember, training in SEL is not the same as training in how to implement a SEL program. The former trains teachers in SEL as a discipline, the latter trains teachers in how to implement the lessons that come with the kit you bought.

PD ideas include:

- on-site (professional learning opportunities, workshops, etc.), including a focus on well-being
- off-site (retreats, certification programs, etc.), including a focus on well-being
- modeling how to use the POP Chart or Thumb Check to check in with every student every day to build interpersonal relationships and human connection (non-instructional time)
- coaching on what explicitly teaching SE competencies looks and sounds like, and how it aligns with current curricula (instructional time)
- SEL 101 training for paraprofessionals, aides, and school stakeholders (wonderful, willing folx that we often leave on the bench when it comes to SEL)

In preparation for that first PD, do your homework. First, invite all educators and caring adults in your school building (paraprofessionals, non-certified staff, etc.) to participate in well-being workshops and SEL trainings. Every adult matters because they are part of the school community *and* because they all teach students how to be in the world. Don't merely give educators permission for well-being ("No longer is the culture of this school one that rewards self-sacrifice..."), be clear about the *times* during their work day when you are giving them space to practice well-being ("The first 20 minutes of our monthly PLC time will be devoted to...") and *when* they are to prioritize SEL over academics ("Non-instructional check-ins should happen each morning for about 3 minutes and SEL should be embedded into instructional content for 10 minutes each day.") Also, let folx know what the expected outcomes will be for their SEL work ("Our projected outcomes are that at least 85% of our students will report that they have a caring relationship with at least one adult in..."), *who* is expected to practice SEL ("SEL is the job of every caring adult in our school who teaches students how to be in the world...") and, finally, if this work will be part of the evaluation process.

Should you survey stakeholders for their input before you speak your expectations? Absolutely! But, who do we need to listen to with the most attention? Our students! We need to listen to the voices (all the voices, not just a few kids on the honor roll who are going to tell us what we want to hear) of the students we support!

Do not delegate this work to a committee of adults who will spend six months creating Google Docs that will make recommendations that ultimately only have weight if they come from you, and are wholly absent of student voice. Your job is to give everyone—adults and students alike—the road map and boundaries in which to do the work. That includes how time will be prioritized and spent. Folx will only feel comfortable spending time on well-being and SEL if they know you will stand by them when that parent calls in to complain about "instructional minutes lost" and they know that their hard work is something that will reflect favorably on their next evaluation.

Thank you for listening, administrators! Lead the way!

Teacher Well-Being: A Lesson for School Administrators on Sources of Stress

It is well-known that teaching is classified as a high-stress career and research over the past several decades supports this (Adams, 2001; Arikewuyo, 2004; Kyriacou, 2001; Milstein & Golaszewski, 1985; Stoeber & Rennert, 2008; Travers & Cooper, 1996; Vandenberghe & Huberman, 1996; Younghusband, Garlie, & Church, 2003). Researchers have found that internal characteristics, such as self-esteem, self-efficacy, and personal behavior, as well as external factors, such as student behavior, workload, work environment, and other colleagues, can contribute to the high level of stress teachers experience on the job (Adams, 2001; Borg, Riding, & Falzon, 1991; Boyle et al., 1995; Collie, Shapka, & Perry, 2012; Roeser,

Skinner, Beers, & Jennings, 2012). These sources lead to burnout, with such symptoms as emotional exhaustion, anxiety, and a lack of motivation, and commitment (Collie, Shapka, & Perry, 2011; Collie et al., 2012; Roeser et al., 2013). Beyond negative implications for teacher well-being, overly stressed teachers can have negative impacts on student performance, behavior, relationships, and their overall ability to meet student needs (Herman, Hickmon-Rosa, & Reinke, 2018; Reinke, Herman, & Stormont, 2013). Negative experiences from teachers and students alike cumulatively contribute to high turnover rates and toxic school climates (Collie et al., 2011; Howard & Johnson, 2004).

Despite the rising prevalence of teacher education programs and professional development on SEL, they scarcely prioritize developing skills related to mindfulness, emotional regulation, and coping with stress for teachers and staff (Roeser et al., 2012, 2013). When schools and districts have implemented programs related to improving social emotional intelligence, they are typically focused on SEL in relation to students and their needs, and less on the SEL impacts and benefits to teachers (Collie et al., 2011; Ransford et al., 2009), though some research proposes that SEL is related to teacher SEC and well-being (Collie et al., 2011; Jennings & Greenberg, 2009).

Existing research suggests that there may be direct and indirect benefits if schools and districts offer mindfulness or SEL training to teachers prior to administering it to students (Roeser et al., 2012; Sarason, 1990). A forthcoming work by Kim, Kakuyama-Vilaber, and Gurolnick (2021) further explores the ways in which students and teachers may directly or indirectly affect one another through the lens of stress and well-being. Their research expands upon existing work by shifting the dynamic to center teacher voice and perception and attempt to gain deeper understanding related to experiences of stress (Collie et al., 2012).

The study utilizes the sample of 975 participants in professional development sessions for SEL during the 2018–2019 school year, which is a part of the implementation framework developed by Mindful Practices, where the first phase focuses on teacher support through professional development and the coaching model. Latent Class Analysis (LCA), which identifies unmeasured patterns of class membership using observed variables (Bowers & Sprott, 2012; Duncan, Duncan, & Strycker, 2006; Goodman, 2002; Urick & Bowers, 2014) determined two classes coupled with two subgroups: The first class finds *Students* to be the main source of stress and *Logistics & Environment* to be the subgroup. This class indicates that one source of stress for teachers stems from student behaviors and needs and this leads to a negative and stressful work environment. It is important to distinguish that our category of *Students* includes both stress from negative student behaviors and stress from a teacher's concerns about their inability to meet a student's needs or help them with personal trauma or struggles. This distinction is significant in order to refine the belief that stress from students is exclusively due to disruptive student behavior. The second class identifies *Logistics & Environment* to be the main source of stress with adult dynamics (both *Management* and *Colleagues*) to be the subgroups. This class indicates that stress stemming from the work environment is largely due to an inability to communicate, collaborate, and work with others including supervisors and administration, in addition to colleagues.

While LCA distinguishes two prominent but separate classes or sources of stress, the results also draw attention to the finding of *Logistics & Environment* as an element of both. This supports past findings and our current suggestions that school and district leaders should be allocating time, efforts, and funding to creating and maintaining a positive school climate that addresses the needs of all people in the building. A last distinction from the findings is that the proportions of the two identified classes indicate that the issues among adults are far more prevalent than those issues from students. These results support the notion that SEL and mindfulness programs should be utilized to improve the well-being of teachers and other school staff, in addition to and potentially even before attending to the social emotional needs of students.

Anna Gurolnick, Reiko Kakuyama-Villaber, and
Dr. Kiljoong Kim, Chapin Hall at the University of Chicago

Appendix

Educator Pre-/Post-Self-Assessment

Name:				Grade:				Date:

Please circle the number that best describes your response.

1. I understand how levels of energy (both my students' and mine) impact my classroom dynamic. I understand the energy and emotions that I am bringing into the classroom.
   1 Strongly disagree   2 Disagree   3 Agree   4 Strongly agree

2. I take the time to understand and address my own well-being needs. I have the resources I need to practice mindfulness, breathing, and/or movement or yoga activities consistently.
   1 Strongly disagree   2 Disagree   3 Agree   4 Strongly agree

3. I honor the well-being needs of my students. We practice (and I model) mindfulness, breathing, and/or movement or yoga activities that help *us* focus, concentrate, and be present in the classroom setting.
   1 Strongly disagree   2 Disagree   3 Agree   4 Strongly agree

4. I regularly embed anti-racist teachings into my lessons. I consistently work on examining my own biases and provide instruction through a culturally responsive lens.
   1 Strongly disagree   2 Disagree   3 Agree   4 Strongly agree

5. I articulate clear, explicit expectations for my students with their SEL work. I understand that students (and adults) have different entry

points to SEL and I provide my instruction through a compassionate and trauma-informed lens.

1 Strongly disagree   2 Disagree   3 Agree   4 Strongly agree

6. I believe it is part of my shared responsibility to make sure that each student has a caring adult to connect with daily, whether it is me or another educator or staff member in the school building.

    1 Strongly disagree   2 Disagree   3 Agree   4 Strongly agree

7. I create a classroom climate that honors student voice and agency and promotes positive youth identity.

    1 Strongly disagree   2 Disagree   3 Agree   4 Strongly agree

8. I model healthy lifestyle choices around food and drink (sugar, caffeine, nutritionally void foods, etc.) for my students.

    1 Strongly disagree   2 Disagree   3 Agree   4 Strongly agree

9. I reflect on my practices as an educator and work hard to develop my own Social Emotional Competency (SEC). I model the behaviors I want my students to exhibit. I *own* that I am a role model.

    1 Strongly disagree   2 Disagree   3 Agree   4 Strongly agree

10. I can communicate with my peers with voice and agency. I can set boundaries with my colleagues, administrators, and my students' parents regarding my time and can effectively manage their expectations.

    1 Strongly disagree   2 Disagree   3 Agree   4 Strongly agree

Educator Questions From the Field

I began Mindful Practices in 2006 to share SEL, mindfulness, yoga, and well-being with students and educators to create deeper human connections. In that time, my team and I have worked with a diverse cohort of schools across the United States and Latin America. The following is a sampling of questions that we often receive. If your question is not answered here, please feel free to contact me directly at carla.p@mindfulpractices.us. I love hearing from readers, as it is important to me that you all have the tools and resources you need to integrate SEL into your classrooms every day.

1. **Problem**: I am the only one implementing SEL at my school. When I approached my principal with this concept she said, "Go ahead and try it; if it works in your room, then we can talk about buying a curriculum next semester." I do not want a curriculum: I want training! How can I develop my own SEC along with my students, if there is no real SEL professional development at my school?

   Solution: First, share the first chapter of this book with your principal. Then, if you are comfortable, ask her if you can facilitate a 20-minute SEL lesson during your next institute day. You can experientially walk your colleagues through a few practices, like Memory Minute and Write/Draw and Rip, and discuss how you use these tools with your students. (You can also share a quick video of your students practicing a POP Check!) Then, offer a follow-up session, online or in-person, for those teachers that are interested in learning more. This is a great way to develop a small community of SEL innovators at your school!

   If you are interested primarily in your growth as a practitioner, try starting a reflective journal on one of these five areas of growth:

   - being explosive or emotionally reactive
   - advocating for personal space and agency
   - being compassionate with self and others
   - navigating difficult conversations
   - wrestling with perfectionism

Try to write in your journal when you are triggered or need a moment to cool down, moving from judgment to observation whenever possible.

2. **Problem**: I only use exercise or yoga videos with my students because my **classroom is so overcrowded**. I would love to use more authentic movement with students as part of their SEL time. How can I get them to stand without being on top of one another? And should I worry about parents' religious objections to yoga or mindfulness?

   Solution: Each and every time you ask the students to stand, explicitly state and model your expectations: *In Room 105 we respect our neighbors' personal space by keeping hands and feet to ourselves. We respect our community by refraining from jokes or comments. And we respect ourselves by listening to our bodies.* As time goes by, this process will become quicker and quicker. Also, always preface that students will have 4 counts to gently pull their chairs out, tuck it in, and stand behind their desks. If they are to return to a seated position, preface that students will have 4 counts to gently pull their chairs out, sit down, and place their hands on their desks. Personal space is a priority at all times.

As for parents' potential religious objections to yoga or mindfulness, it is always best to err on the side of caution and send a note home to parents, explaining that yoga is the union of body and mind and that mindfulness is a practice that helps us be in the present moment. Reassure them that no religion will be taught, but explain that the students will be moving through poses and that parents should let the school know if they or the student are uncomfortable so that alternative accommodations can be made.

3. **Problem**: I love using movement to energize my class, but I teach students with limited physical mobility. Is there a class song or cheer I can use to energize my class that can be practiced from their seats?

   Solution: Try this class song, sung to the tune of "The Rubber Ducky Song"

   Room 204
   You're the one
   You make school lots of fun
   Room 204 I'm awfully found of YOU
   Boo boo be do!

> *Room 204*
> *You're full of heart*
> *You try your best and you're really smart*
> *Room 204 you're a really great class it's true boo boo be do!*

4. **Problem**: I am an administrator and I want to **start our day with a positive** breathing activity to build our school climate and culture. Any ideas?

    Solution: Say the following as part of the announcements every morning.

    > We try our best.
    > We are self-aware.
    > We are responsible for our own behavior.
    > We matter.
    > We are the Solution!

Then, roll into "We are—We are—the Solution (clap clap)!—the Solution (clap clap)! We are—We are—the Solution (clap clap)! The Solution (clap clap)!"

(Sung to the tune of "We Will Rock You.")

Depending on teachers' comfort levels, you can ask them to have students clap or pound on desks as a great way to let go of excess energy.

To begin class with centered energy, conclude the activity with a Memory Minute.

5. **Problem**: I am a school administrator and I need more ideas on including *be the solution*, our **Call to Action**, across the school. I am having a hard time getting our classroom aides and staff to buy into it.

    Solution: Invite your **school community** to get involved in the school's daily routines, such as morning announcements. "Mahwah School, let's start our day the be the solution Way!"

School stakeholders are the faces that shape your students' educational experiences. This includes classroom teachers, bus drivers, specials teachers, custodians, cafeteria staff, social workers, recess staff, parents, and community members.

"Our students are everyone's responsibility. Each role has value." No one in the school is viewed as a babysitter or an "invisible" cog in the system. Each person is valued and each person is expected to model be the solution behavior and messaging for the students.

6. **Problem**: I love using a Call to Action to get students motivated! Can I have a few more examples of **how it can help transitions** when time is tight?

    Solution: Room 314 is working in centers when the fire alarm goes off. By the time the students return to their classroom, there are only 2 minutes remaining before dismissal. Mr. Caillou, the teacher, needs the room cleaned up before the students line up for the bus.

Mr. Caillou announces, "OK Room 314, it is time to **be the solution**!" He moves swiftly to the board and writes the following:

Be the solution: Cleaning up after group work
Time start: 11:04
Time stop: 11:06

Alternatively, a teacher senses that her class is really nervous. She wants them to practice a quick activity to get centered and focused.

"OK class, we need to focus before we move to the rug for Come Together Time. Lee Sun Yew, will you select an activity from the POP Chart that will help our class focus?" Once the activity has been chosen, the teacher writes the time and activity on the board.

Be in the zone: Focus
Activity: Memory Moment
Time start: 1:02
Time stop: 1:03

Lee Sun Yew facilitates the activity and the teacher acts as timer.

7. **Problem**: I need a few more examples of how I can use **both structured and unstructured** movement with my students. Also, I never know what type of music to play for them. Any ideas?

    Solution: Practicing movement prior to group work is a great way to help the class release excess energy that can often make being present and focused challenging for your more frenetic students.

For a structured approach, ask one of your students to volunteer to lead a sequence of physical movements appropriate for the layout of your classroom. You can write a sample sequence on the board, such as:

    Starfish Pose (five breaths)
    Tree Pose (five breaths, right side)
    Starfish Pose (five breaths)
    Tree Pose (five breaths, left side)
    Seated Arm Stretch (count of 10)

For **a less structured approach** or when working with a reluctant group, put on music and declare Free Dance for the next 90 seconds. Students can move in whatever way they feel comfortable (fast or slow, subtle, or grand), as long as they are respecting their neighbor's personal space and using moves appropriate for school (i.e., no fighting gestures, miming sexual positions, or fake firing of weapons). When you feel the students' energy starting to shift ask the students to slowly find their seats. Once they are seated, close the session with a centering activity like Color Breath.

For music, my Mindful Practices team created a fun Motown playlist to use with student and adult learners. It is upbeat and always a hit!

    "The Way You Do the Things You Do" (The Temptations)
    "Superstition" (Stevie Wonder)
    "You Can't Hurry Love" (The Supremes)
    "Please Mr. Postman" (The Marvelettes)
    "Think" (Aretha Franklin)
    "Hold On, I'm Coming" (Sam & Dave)
    "Lovely Day" (Bill Withers)

These songs are probably already on your classroom playlist. I hear them in lots of early childhood classrooms I visit.

    "The More We Get Together" (Raffi)
    "Head, Shoulders, Knees and Toes"
    "Getting to Know Myself" (Hap Palmer)
    "Clean Up Song" (Singing Walrus)
    "Clean Up is Fun" (Learning Station)
    "Make a Circle"

"Everybody Take a Seat" (Jbrary)
"Open, Shut Them" (Intellidance)
"Hello, How Are You" (Kiboomers)
"Goodbye Song for the Classroom" (DJC Kids)
"If You're Happy and You Know It" (Twinkle Songs)
"What Do People Do" (Hap Palmer)

Bibliography

Acedo, C., Opertti, R., Brady, J., & Duncombe, L. (2011). *Interregional and regional perspectives on inclusive education: Follow-up of the 48th session of the international conference on education*. Paris: United Nations Educational, Scientific and Cultural Organization.

Adams, E. (2001). A proposed causal model of vocational teacher stress. *Journal of Vocational Education and Training, 53*(2), 223–246.

Adams, J. (2017). *The ABC of mindfulness*. Retrieved from www.mindfulnet.org

Albright, M. I., & Weissberg, R. P. (2010). School—family partnerships to promote social and emotional learning. In S. L. Christenson & A. L. Reschly (Eds.), *Handbook of school—family partnerships* (pp. 246–265). New York: Routledge.

Arikewuyo, M. O. (2004). Stress management strategies of secondary school teachers in Nigeria. *Educational Research, 46*, 195–207.

Barrera, M., Biglan, A., Taylor, T. K., Gunn, B. K., Smolkowski, K., Black, C., Ary, D. V., & Fowler, R. C. (2002). Early elementary school intervention to reduce conduct problems: A randomized trial with hispanic and non-hispanic children. *Prevention Science, 3*(2), 83–94.

Biffle, C. (2013). *Whole brain teaching for challenging kids (and the rest of your class, too!)*. Yucaipa, CA: Whole Brain Teaching LLC.

Borg, M. G., Riding, R. J., & Falzon, J. M. (1991). Stress in teaching: A study of occupational stress and its determinants, job satisfaction and career commitment among primary school teachers. *Educational Psychology, 11*, 59–75.

Bowers, A. J., & Sprott, R. (2012). Examining the multiple trajectories associated with dropping out of high school: A growth mixture model analysis. *Journal of Educational Research, 105*, 176–195.

Boyle, G. J., Borg, M. G., Falzon, J. M., & Baglioni, J., & Anthony, J. (1995). A structural model of the dimensions of teacher stress. *British Journal of Educational Psychology, 65*(1), 49–67.

Brown, B. (2010). *The gifts of imperfection: Let go of who you think you're supposed to be and embrace who you are*. Center City, MI: Hazelden.

Butzer, B., Bury, D., Telles, S., & Khalsa, S. B. S. (2016). Implementing yoga within the school curriculum: A scientific rationale for improving social-emotional learning and positive student outcomes. *Journal of Children's Services*, *11*(1), 3–24.

Chicago Public Schools (CPS). (2017). *School quality rating policy*. Retrieved from www.cps.edu/Performance/Pages/PerformancePolicy.aspx

Chödrön, P. (2020). *Welcoming the unwelcome: Wholehearted living in a brokenhearted world*. Boulder, CO: Shambhala.

Collaborative for Academic, Social, and Emotional Learning (CASEL). (2020). Retrieved from www.casel.org

Collie, R. J., Shapka, J. D., & Perry, N. E. (2011). Predicting teacher commitment: The impact of school climate and social-emotional learning. *Psychology in the Schools*, *48*(10), 1034–1048. doi: 10.1002/pits.20611

Collie, R. J., Shapka, J. D., & Perry, N. E. (2012). School climate and social–emotional learning: Predicting teacher stress, job satisfaction, and teaching efficacy. *Journal of Educational Psychology*, *104*(4), 1189–1204. doi:10.1037/a0029356

Cook-Cottone, C. P. (2015). *Mindfulness and yoga for self-regulation: A primer for mental health professionals*. New York: Springer.

Danielson, C., & Chicago Public Schools (CPS). (2011). *CPS framework for teaching companion guide: Version 1.0*. Chicago: CPS.

Duncan, T., Duncan, S., & Strycker, L. (2006). *An introduction to latent variable growth curve modeling: Concepts, issues, and applications*. Mahwah, NJ: Lawrence Erlbaum.

Durlak, J. A., Weissberg, R. P., Dymnicki, A. B., Taylor, R. D., & Schellinger, K. B. (2011). The impact of enhancing students' social and emotional learning: A meta-analysis of school-based universal interventions. *Child Development*, *82*(1), 405–432.

Farhi, D. (1996). *The breathing book: Good health and vitality through essential breath work*. New York: Henry Holt.

Farrington, C. A., Roderick, M., Allensworth, E., Nagaoka, J., Keyes, T. S., Johnson, D. W., & Beechum, N. O. (2012). *Teaching adolescents to become learners* (pp. 1–102). Chicago, IL: University of Chicago Consortium on Chicago School Research Literature Review.

Fisher, E. P. (1992). The impact of play on development: A meta-analysis. *Play and Culture*, *5*(2), 159–181.

Forbes, H. T. (2013). Teaching trauma in the classroom. *Focus on Adoption*, *21*(4), 27.

Friedman, J., & Boumil, M. (1995). *Betrayal of trust: Sex and power in professional relationships*. Westport, CT: Praeger.

Froh, J., & Bono, G. (2014). *Seven ways to foster gratitude in kids*. Berkeley, CA: The Greater Good Science Center.

Fullan, M. (2011). *Change leader: Learning to do what matters most*. San Francisco, CA: Jossey-Bass.

Goleman, D., & Senge, P. (2014). *The triple focus: A new approach to education.* Florence, MA: More Than Sound.

Goodman, L. (2002). Latent class analysis: The empirical study of latent types, latent variables, and latent structures. In J. Hagennaars & A. McCutcheon (Eds.), *Applied latent class analysis* (pp. 3–55). Cambridge: Cambridge University Press.

Greene, R. W. (2014). *Lost at school: Why our kids with behavioral challenges are falling through the cracks and how we can help them.* New York: Scribner.

Hackney, P. (2002). *Making connections: Total body integration through Bartenieff fundamentals.* New York: Routledge.

Hargreaves, A., & Fullan, M. (2012). *Professional capital: Transforming teaching in every school.* New York: Teachers College Press.

Harrison, L. J., Manocha, R., & Rubia, K. S. (2004). Yoga meditation as a family treatment for children with attention deficit—hyperactivity disorder. *Clinical Child Psychology and Psychiatry, 9,* 479–497.

Hattie, J. (2009). *Visible learning: A synthesis of over 800 meta-analyses relating to achievement.* New York: Routledge.

Herman, K. C., Hickmon-Rosa, J. E., & Reinke, W. M. (2018). Empirically derived profiles of teacher stress, burnout, self-efficacy, and coping and associated student outcomes. *Journal of Positive Behavior Interventions, 20*(2), 90–100.

Howard, S., & Johnson, B. (2004). Resilient teachers: Resisting stress and burnout. *Social Psychology of Education, 7,* 399–420. doi: 10.1007/s11218-004-0975-0

Illinois State Board of Education (ISBE). (2006). *Special education and support services: Service learning guide.* Retrieved from www.isbe.state.il.us

Illinois State Board of Education (ISBE). (2013). *Illinois early learning and development standards.* Retrieved from www.isbe.state.il.us

Illinois State Board of Education (ISBE). (n.d.). *Social-emotional learning standards.* Retrieved from www.isbe.state.il.us

Jennings, P. A., & Greenberg, M. T. (2009). The prosocial classroom: Teacher social and emotional competence in relation to student and classroom outcomes. *Review of Educational Research, 79,* 491–525. doi: 10.3102/0034654308325693

Jha, A. P., Krompinger, J., & Baime, M. J. (2007). Mindfulness training modifies subsystems of attention. *Journal of Cognitive Affective and Behavioral Neuroscience, 7,* 109–119.

Jones, D. (2007). Healthy and smart: Using wellness to boost performance. *Principal Leadership, 8*(4), 32–36.

Jones, S., Bouffard, S., & Weissbourd, R. (2013). Educators' social and emotional skills vital to learning. *Kappan Magazine, 94*(8), 62–65.

Kabat-Zinn, J. (1990). *Full catastrophe living: Using the wisdom of your body and mind to face stress, pain and illness.* New York: Dell.

Kabat-Zinn, J. (2016). Awareness has no center and no periphery. *Mindfulness,* 7(5), 1241–1242.

Kim, K., Kakuyama-Villaber, R., & Gurolnick, A. (2021). *Sources of work-related stress for teachers and school staff.* Manuscript in Preparation.

Kripalu Center for Yoga and Health. (2015). *Kripalu yoga in the schools curriculum.* Stockbridge, MA: Kripalu.

Kyriacou, C. (2001). Teacher Stress; directions for future research. *Educational Review, 53,* 27–35.

Lawlor, M. S. (2014). Mindfulness in practice: Considerations for implementation of mindfulness-based programming for adolescents in school contexts. *New Directions for Youth Development, 142,* 83–95.

Lemov, D. (2010). *Teach like a champion: 49 techniques that put students on the path to college.* San Francisco, CA: Jossey-Bass.

Linden, W. (1973). Practicing of meditation by school children and their levels of field dependence-independence, test anxiety and reading achievement. *Journal of Consulting and Clinical Psychology, 41,* 139–143.

McKinley, J. (2010). *Raising Black students' achievement through culturally responsive teaching.* Alexandria, VA: Association for Supervision and Curriculum Development.

Miller, J. (2015, June 15). The power of parenting with social and emotional learning. *Huffington Post.*

Milstein, M., & Golaszewski, T. (1985). Effect of organizationally based and individually based stress management efforts in elementary school sittings. *Urban Education, 19*(4), 389–409.

National Child Traumatic Stress Network Schools Committee. (2008). *Child trauma toolkit for educators.* Los Angeles, CA and Durham, NC: National Center for Child Traumatic Stress. Retrieved from www.nctsnet.org/sites/default/files/assets/pdfs/Child_Trauma_Toolkit_Final.pdf

Nuthall, G. A. (1999). Learning how to learn: The evolution of students' minds through the social processes and culture of the classroom. *International Journal of Educational Research, 31*(3), 141–256.

Patrick, S. D., Tsukayama, E., & Duckworth, A. L. (2014, April). *A tripartite taxonomy of character.* Paper presented at the annual meeting of the American Education Research Association, Philadelphia, PA.

Purcell, M., & Murphy, J. (2014). *Mindfulness for teen anger.* Oakland, CA: New Harbinger Publications.

Ransford, C. R., Greenberg, M. T., Domitrovich, C. E., Small, M., & Jacobson, L. (2009). The role of teachers' psychological experiences and perceptions of curriculum supports on the implementation of a social and emotional learning curriculum. *School Psychology Review, 38*(4), 510–532.

Reinke, W. M., Herman, K. C., & Stormont, M. (2013). Classroom-level positive behavior supports in schools implementing SW-PBIS: Identifying areas for enhancement. *Journal of Positive Behavior Interventions, 15,* 39–50.

Roeser, R. W., & Peck, S. C. (2009). An education in awareness: Self, motivation, and self-regulated learning in contemplative perspective. *Educational Psychologist, 44*(2), 119–136.

Roeser, R. W., Schonert-Reichl, K. A., Jha, A., Cullen, M., Wallace, L., Wilensky, R., . . . Harrison, J. (2013). Mindfulness training and reductions in teacher stress and burnout: Results from two randomized, waitlist-control field trials. *Journal of Educational Psychology, 105*(3), 787.

Roeser, R. W., Skinner, E., Beers, J., & Jennings, P. A. (2012). Mindfulness training and teachers' professional development: An emerging area of research and practice. *Child Development Perspectives, 6*(2), 167–173.

Rubin, G. (2011). *The happiness project.* New York: HarperCollins.

Sarason, S. B. (1990). *The predictable failure of school reform.* San Francisco, CA: Jossey-Bass.

Senge, P., Cambron-McCabe, N., Lucas, T., Smith, B., Dutton, J., & Kleiner, A. (2012). *Schools that learn: A fifth discipline fieldbook for educators, parents, and everyone who cares about education.* New York: Crown Business.

Serwacki, M., & Cook-Cottone, C. (2012). Yoga in the schools: A systematic review of the literature. *International Journal of Yoga Therapy, 22*(1), 101–110.

Shechtman, N., DeBarger, A., Dornsife, C., Rosier, S., & Yarnall, L. (2013, February 14). *Promoting grit, tenacity, and perseverance: Critical factors for success in the 21st century.* Menlo Park, CA: U.S. Department of Education Office of Educational Technology.

Siegel, R. (2014). *The science of mindfulness: A research-based path to wellbeing.* The Great Courses, Audio. London: Taylor & Francis.

Social and Emotional Learning. (2020, December 8). *American institutes for research.* Retrieved from www.air.org/topic/education/social-and-emotional-learning

Sparrowe, L. (2011, Fall). Transcending trauma. *Yoga International,* 48–53, 89.

Spolin, V. (1986). *Theater games for the classroom: A teacher's handbook.* Chicago, IL: Northwestern University Press.

Stoeber, J., & Rennert, D. (2008). Perfectionism in school teachers: relations with stress sppraisals, coping styles, and burnout. *Anxiety, Stress, & Coping, 21,* 37–53.

Strong, W. B., Malina, R. M., Blimkie, C. J. R., Daniels, S. R., Dushman, R. K., Gutin, B., . . . Trudeau, F. (2005). Evidence based physical activity for school-age youth. *The Journal of Pediatrics, 146*(6), 732–737.

Stueck, M., & Gloeckner, N. (2005). Yoga for children in the mirror of the science: Working spectrum and practice fields of the training of relaxation with elements of yoga for children. *Early Child Development and Care, 175*(4), 371–377.

Tantillo Philibert, C. (2016). *Everyday SEL in elementary school*. London: Routledge.

Tantillo Philibert, C., & Crowley, E. (2012). *Cooling down your classroom: Using yoga, relaxation and breathing strategies to help students learn to keep their cool*. Chicago, IL: Mindful Practices.

Tantillo Philibert, C., Soto, C., & Veon, L. (2020). *Everyday self-care for educators: Tools and strategies for well-being*. New York: Routledge.

Trauma and Learning Policy Initiative. (2013). *Helping traumatized children learn, volume 2: Creating and advocating for trauma-sensitive schools*. Retrieved from https://traumasensitiveschools.org/tlpi-publications/download-a-free-copy-of-a-guide-to-creating-trauma-sensitive-schools/

Travers, C. J., & Cooper, C. L. (1996). *Teachers under pressure: Stress in the teacher profession*. London: Routledge.

Urick, A., & Bowers, A. J. (2014). What are the different types of principals across the United States? A latent class analysis of principal perception of leadership. *Educational Administration Quarterly, 50*(1), 96–134.

van der Kolk, B. (2014). *The body keeps the score*. New York: Penguin Books.

Vandenberghe, R., & Huberman, A. M. (1996). *Understanding and preventing teacher burnout: A sourcebook of international research and practice*. Cambridge: Cambridge UP.

Wessler, S., & Preble, W. (2003). *The respectful school: How educators and students can conquer hate and harassment*. Alexandria, VA: Association for Supervision and Curriculum Development.

Willard, C. (2014). *Mindfulness for teen anxiety*. Oakland, CA: Instant Help Publications.

Williams, M. & Penman, D. (2011). *Mindfulness: An eight-week plan for finding peace in a frantic world*. Macmillan Audio.

Wong, H. K. (2009). *Facilitator's handbook: The effective teacher*. Mountain View, CA: Harry K. Wong Publications.

Wong, H. K., & Wong, R. T. (2009). *The first days of school: How to be an effective teacher*. Mountain View, CA: Harry K. Wong Publications.

Younghusband, L., Garlie, N., & Church, E. (2003). *High school teacher stress in Newfoundland, Canada*. Paper presented at the International Conference on Education, Hawaii.

For Product Safety Concerns and Information please contact our EU representative GPSR@taylorandfrancis.com
Taylor & Francis Verlag GmbH, Kaufingerstraße 24, 80331 München, Germany